My Own Red Roses

My Own Red Roses

G. A. Hodcroft

The Book Guild Limited
SUSSEX ENGLAND

for MARY,
the most tolerant and understanding of 'cricket widows'

and

PETER,
who shared many enjoyable days in the sun.

The Book Guild Limited
Temple House, 25 High Street,
Lewes, Sussex

First published 1984
©G. A. Hodcroft 1984

Set in Linotron Bembo

Made and printed in Great Britain by
Antony Rowe Ltd.
Chippenham

ISBN 0 86332 020 1

Acknowledgements

I am indebted for much valuable information about the earlier Lancashire cricketers I never saw play and those I saw briefly in tender, uninformed years, to the two histories of the County Club by A. W. Ledbrooke and Rex Pogson and to the Club's own centenary publication, 'A Hundred Years of Cricket, 1864–1964'. No writer on Lancashire cricket and cricketers can fail to be grateful to the writings of Sir Neville Cardus whose felicitous essays are part of the rich heritage of the game.

I am grateful also to Mr. R. Warburton, Assistant Secretary of the Lancashire County Cricket Club for his ready help in providing many of the photographs and to Mr. Reg. Parkin for permission to quote his father's limerick.

Acknowledgement is made by the publishers and myself to copyright holders of illustrations for permission to reproduce them in this book. In some cases, though every effort has been made, it has not been possible to contact original copyright holders and we apologise for any lack of attribution or permission.

B

Illustrations appear between pages 60 and 61 and
between pages 92 and 93

Contents

AT LORD'S

It is little I repair to the matches of the Southron folk,
Though my own red roses there may blow;
It is little I repair to the matches of the Southron folk,
Though the red roses crest the caps, I know.
For the field is full of shades as I near the shadowy coast,
And a ghostly batsman plays to the bowling of a ghost,
And I look through my tears on a soundless-clapping host
As the run-stealers flicker to and fro,
　　　　To and fro:–
O my Hornby and my Barlow long ago!

Francis Thompson. (1857–1907)

I

The Early Days

The game of cricket was flourishing in the Manchester area in the early years of the nineteenth century and there is evidence aplenty of matches arranged between local sides before the formation of the Manchester Club in 1818. In the earliest days of its existence the Club played its matches first at the Crescent in Salford, and subsequently at Moss Lane, Hulme. An 1826 scorebook carries the details of a game played between Manchester and a Garrison side made up from units of the Coldstream Guards and the Queen's Bays. In those days, apparently, obstruction was recorded much more precisely than was later to become the custom and the book reveals that one of the batsmen was dismissed 'foot before wicket'.

In 1842 the members of the Club decided to raise their ambition beyond the horizon of the Manchester hinterland, and with commendable optimism a team was despatched to Lord's to play against the Gentlemen of the all-powerful Marylebone Cricket Club. Unfortunately on this occasion, London was to learn nothing from the northern cricketers, and the game was conceded by the challengers after the M.C.C. had scored 220 in reply to Manchester's first innings total of 59. It would seem that the Gentlemen of the M.C.C., accustomed to much sterner challenges, were more than a little amused by the rawness of the Manchester bowling, which at that time consisted entirely of underarm deliveries, and they had no difficulty in despatching it to all quarters of the field.

The Lord's visit must at least have taught the Mancunians that they should develop the round-arm bowling which had been permissible since 1828 if their cricket ambitions were to be taken seriously.

Two years later they met and defeated an All-Yorkshire side and in 1847 the standard of Manchester cricket must have been considered sufficiently improved for the Club to entertain the famous All-England Eleven which was touring under its formid-

able captain, George Parr. Parr was in tremendous form with the
bat, and against a field of eighteen or more, it is recorded that he
followed up innings of 100 at Leicester and 78 not out at York
with 64 at Manchester, on each occasion the highest score of the
game.

As the City of Manchester expanded and developed it became
necessary for the Club to seek a new ground. A suitable site was
found at Old Trafford close to the Royal Botanical Gardens, a
site roughly approximating to that now occupied by the White
City Stadium on the main Chester Road. Here, in 1847, a pitch
was laid out and in the same year, for the first time, matches were
organized between teams representing Lancashire and Yorkshire, the first at Sheffield and the second at Old Trafford.

In 1856 the ground site was required for an Art and Treasures
Exhibition, and though the officials of the Club attempted to
resist the threatened eviction, they were unsuccessful. Fortunately an alternative site was available close at hand, and the Old
Trafford cricket ground was established where it stands today.

In *Bell's Life* of 28th June, 1857, the opening fixture – Manchester v Liverpool – was reported thus:-

OPENING OF THE
MANCHESTER NEW CRICKET GROUND.

'The ground which, for many years, was occupied by the
Manchester Cricket Club at Old Trafford, is now covered by
the Art and Treasures Palace. The new ground is situated to
the west of the Exhibition buildings, and consists of about
eight acres of good, level, sandy land. The pavilion is erected
on the north side; and while it is a great ornament to the
ground, it is well adapted for the purposes for which it will be
used. It consists of a centre compartment (intended for a dining
hall) and two wings, a turret surmounting the centre. The
dining hall is 36 feet long by 22 feet wide. Underneath the
building is an excellent wine cellar, no unimportant acquisi-
tion in a cricket pavilion. The entire front of the dining hall,
which commands a view of the whole field, is composed of
glass.

Manchester won the two innings game by 31 runs.

In 1863, across the Pennines, the Yorkshire County Club was
established, and a year later, members of the Manchester Club
invited other prominent Lancastrians to a meeting at the Queens

Hotel, Manchester to consider the desirability of forming a County Cricket Club, with, as the *Blackburn Standard* of 20th January, 1864 reported, 'A view of spreading a thorough knowledge and appreciation of the game throughout Lancashire.' The meeting attracted amateur cricketers from all parts of Lancashire. It was proposed that matches would be played in Manchester, Preston, Blackburn and other towns in the County. The recommended annual subscription was to be one guinea, and it was felt to be desirable that whatever surplus might remain after the payment of expenses, should be funded so that at some future date a ground and accommodation could be secured that would answer all the requirements of the County's cricket.

In 1864 Wisden published his first *Cricketer's Almanac*, but curiously this first edition makes no mention of Lancashire cricket or of the formation of the County Club.

The first match in which an official Lancashire team took part was played at Warrington on June 15th and 16th, 1864. Birkenhead Park and Ground provided the opposition and Lancashire were represented by an all-amateur eleven. Though Lancashire led on the first innings by 26 runs, they were saved from defeat only by the running out of time, for they were dismissed for 78 in their second innings and Birkenhead Park were 90 for one wicket at the drawing of stumps. There were also games against the Gentlemen of Shropshire at Liverpool and Shrewsbury, the Gentlemen of Warwickshire at Warwick and Old Trafford and the Gentlemen of Yorkshire at Broughton and York.

The laudable intention of playing games all over Lancashire soon foundered for not only did there grow up a disinclination to move fixtures away from Old Trafford, but the formation of the Lancashire League provided alternative matches for players and public and the County Club was sometimes frustrated in its wishes to engage certain players for its fixtures.

The first inter-county match was played at Old Trafford on July 20th, 21st and 22nd, 1865, when Middlesex were the visitors. Contrary to expectations the game was poorly supported by the general public and the gate receipts totalled less than £25. If the public showed little interest the historians must pay it more attention for in Lancashire's second innings, after a first innings tie, V.E. Walker took all ten wickets. His remarkable performance, however, did not prevent Lancashire winning by 62 runs.

Lancashire

1st INNINGS

R. Blackstock	c & b. Wilkinson		18
F.J. Cooke	b. R.D. Walker		35
R. Iddison	b Howitt		20
J.F. Leese	c & b Howitt		33
J. Makinson	b. T. Hearne		45
E. Whittaker	c. Haines	b. Wilkinson	23
E. Bousfield	c. V.E. Walker	b. T. Hearne	0
A.B. Rowley	c. Wilkinson	b. T. Hearne	24
S.H. Swire	NOT OUT		18
W. Perry	c. Morley	b. Catling	16
F. Reynolds	c. T. Hearne	b. Catling	9
Extras			2
			243

2nd INNINGS

R. Blackstock	b. V.E. Walker		5
F.J. Cooke	St. Morley	b. V.E. Walker	20
R. Iddison	c & b. V.E. Walker		6
J.F. Leese	c. Haines	b. V.E. Walker	0
J. Makinson	St. Morley	b. V.E. Walker	0
E. Whittaker	c. R.D. Walker	b. V.E. Walker	39
E. Bousfield	c. Wilkinson	b. V.E. Walker	15
A.B. Rowley	c. R.D. Walker	b. V.E. Walker	60
S.H. Swire	b. V.E. Walker		16
W. Perry	c & b. V.E. Walker		0
F. Reynolds	NOT OUT		13
Extras			4
			178

Middlesex
1st INNINGS

A.J. Wilkinson	c. Blackstock	b. Iddison	59
J. Haines	b. Iddison		3
B. Robertson	St. Perry	b. Iddison	13
R.D. Walker	c. Perry	b. Rowley	84
T. Hearne	c. Makinson	b. Rowley	26
V.E. Walker	c & b. Reynolds		0
G. Hearne	c. Perry	b. Rowley	14
W. Catling	b. Reynolds		3
T. Mantle	lbw.	b. Reynolds	0
G. Howitt	RUN OUT		23
J.H. Morley	NOT OUT		6
Extras			12
			243

2nd INNINGS

A.J. Wilkinson	Absent		0
J. Haines	RUN OUT		3
B. Robertson	c. Reynolds	b. Iddison	3
R. D. Walker	b. Reynolds		28
T. Hearne	c. Bousefield	b. Iddison	5
V.E. Walker	c. Perry	b. Iddison	29
G. Hearne	c. Leese	b. Reynolds	14
W. Catling	NOT OUT		0
T. Mantle	c. Leese	b. Iddison	4
G. Howitt	b. Iddison		5
J.H. Morley	b. Reynolds		19
Extras			6
			116

In this game the Lancashire side was composed of eight

amateurs and three professionals, Iddison, Perry and Reynolds. Some counties, notably Yorkshire, Notts and Surrey were, at this period, including a fair sprinkling of professionals in their teams, but for the first twenty years of its existence the Lancashire County Club relied very largely on amateur players.

S.H.Swire and A.B.Rowley were later to play considerable parts on the administrative side at Old Trafford. Rowley subsequently became President of the Club and Swire served as Honorary Secretary continuously from 1869 to 1905. A fine portrait in oils of Swire, the patriarch of Lancashire cricket hangs in the long room of the pavilion, his eyes looking out over the ground, to the well-being of which he devoted a great part of his time and energy.

Fred Reynolds was a 'character' in his own right, and when his playing days were done he served the Club in the capacity of groundsman, coach, assistant secretary and subscription collector. Stories about him are legion. He was something of a connoisseur of whisky and it is said that he secreted in a remote part of the pavilion a cache of the spirit, the existence of which was known to no one but himself. During alterations to the pavilion the precious hoard was discovered by workmen in the temporary absence of Reynolds (possibly on one of his subscription-hunting expeditions) and work was temporarily suspended whilst the finders sampled what they had plainly decided was their legitimate right. The temporary suspension became more permanent as the raw spirit took effect and when Fred returned from his labours, doubtless feeling in need of a little refreshment himself, he found the workmen all sound asleep, expressions of the utmost contentment on their faces and their slumbering bodies surrounded by empty bottles. Fred was never one to mince his words and the hubbub he raised was terrifying to hear.

Fred always preferred the personal approach in his subscription collecting. Not for him the intermediary intervention of Her Majesty's Postal Service. He reckoned that time was saved if he called on members at their various places of business, and once in an office, he very rarely left without a drop of something to sustain him on his way. The sustenance would frequently not be confined to a single glass, for Fred had a wonderful repertoire of anecdotes and reminiscences and he was a past master in the art of communicating to his listeners the fact that his throat had become parched in the telling of his stories.

In 1866 home and away games were played with Middlesex and Surrey, and in 1867 the long rivalry with Yorkshire began with a match at Whalley played on 20th, 21st and 22nd June. Lancashire were easily beaten by an innings and 56 runs:-

LANCASHIRE

1st Innings

A.N. Hornby	c. Stevenson	b. Freeman	2
J. Ricketts	b. Greenwood		3
J.F. Leese	c. Freeman	b. Greenwood	22
C. Coward	b. Greenwood		13
A.B. Rowley	b. Greenwood		0
G. Holgate	c. Anderson	b. Freeman	8
A. Appleby	b. Freeman		1
W. Hickton	c. Anderson	b. Freeman	2
E. Leventon	b. Freeman		0
E.B. Rawlinson	NOT OUT		1
- Hibbert	b. Freeman		2
Extras			3
		Total	57

2nd INNINGS

A.N. Hornby	b. Freeman		3
J. Ricketts	b. Freeman		0
J.F. Leese	b. Freeman		4
C. Coward	c. Iddison	b. Greenwood	5
A.B. Rowley	b. Freeman		0
G. Holgate	RUN OUT		21
A. Appleby	b. Greenwood		18
W. Hickton	b. Freeman		0
E. Leventon	c. Iddison	b. Greenwood	6
E.B. Rawlinson	b. Greenwood		14
- Hibbert	NOT OUT		2
Extras			2
		Total	75

YORKSHIRE

J. Rowbotham	c. Hornby	b. Appleby	7
J. Thewlis	b. Appleby		1
E. Stevenson	b. Leventon		54
R. Iddison	b. Appleby		14

J.E. Lee	b. Appleby		0
E. Dawson	b. Hickton		11
G. Anderson	b. Leventon		6
G. Freeman	c. Rawlinson	b. Hickton	28
J. Berry	c. Hibbert	b. Appleby	27
L. Greenwood	c & b. Appleby		19
G. Atkinson	NOT OUT		14
Extras			7
		Total	188

It is of interest to note that R. Iddison who was playing for Yorkshire in this match was the same R. Iddison who had turned out for Lancashire against Middlesex the previous year. The rules governing the qualification of players were not so strict in those early days, and in the following season Iddison played for Lancashire against Surrey. He was then claimed by Yorkshire, but in 1868 he was turning out again for Lancashire, achieving the distinction of hitting the first century scored for the County (106 against Surrey at the Oval).

Gideon Holgate, who also played for Lancashire in the game at Whalley, was another Yorkshireman who turned out for both counties; his appearance under the red rose banner in that first 'roses' match in 1867 was followed by two appearances for Yorkshire against his former Lancastrian colleagues.

William Hickton, a Derbyshire man and a fast round-arm bowler rendered sterling service to the Lancashire Club in the years between 1867 and 1871, but when the two counties met in the latter year, Hickton transferred his allegiance to the county of his birth and played a not inconsiderable part in Lancashire's defeat.

There were other glaring examples of cricketers playing for more than one county side. Four Hornby brothers were included in a Gentlemen of Cheshire side which played the Gentlemen of Lancashire at Chelford in 1866. Less than a month later, A.N. and E.K. Hornby were playing for the Gentlemen of Lancashire against the Gentlemen of Yorkshire.

Some system of qualification was obviously desirable if competitive county cricket were not to assume the aspect of a war conducted by mercenaries, and in 1873, with the institution of the County Championship, formal rules were drawn up.

A.N. Hornby made his first appearance in the County side in

1867, and though his record in that first 'roses' match at Whalley was not exactly auspicious, he began to assert himself and ultimately achieved a dominance which saw him at the head of the batting averages each season from 1869 to 1872. It was the start of a long and fruitful association with Lancashire cricket which lasted until his death in 1925.

Reynolds, Hickton and Holgate were the principal professionals in those early days, but the Club relied mainly on its amateur talent. Besides the Hornbys, the Rowleys and the Hultons, the names which recur again and again in the early score-books and records are those of J.F. Leese, E. Whittaker, E. Challender, E. Moorhouse, E. Roper, F. Rutter, F.W. Wright, A. Appleby and E.J. Bousfield. *Lillywhite's Annual*, referring to the 1871 season, however, had this to say of Lancashire cricket – 'There is no lack of cricketers in the county, but they are irregular in their support and their defection is at times disastrous. Probably more recourse to professionals will have a better effect.'

The hint was taken. Alec Watson and R.G. Barlow joined the professional ranks and they were soon followed by William McIntyre from Nottingham. The effect was propitious. Yorkshire and Derbyshire were defeated twice and there was a new air of confidence at Old Trafford. A year later Hornby and Barlow began their famous association.

II

Hornby and Barlow

Albert Neilson Hornby, nicknamed 'Monkey', an old Harrovian, was to be a force in Lancashire cricket for the next half century. In one of his eloquent essays Sir Neville Cardus writes of 'the breeze that was Hornby blowing over Old Trafford.' In his prime 'Monkey' Hornby was assuredly much more of a gale than a breeze.

He was born in Blackburn in 1847, but he first came to the notice of cricketing circles when he played in the Harrow team at Lord's. It was said at that time that he was the smallest cricketer ever seen on the ground. One authority has it that he weighed under six stone, including his bat, but even at that early stage of his career he was possessed of an abundant energy and he had the penchant for stealing short singles which was to be the despair of his batting partners throughout his cricketing life. It was this run-stealing which was to raise Hornby to immortality in the lines of the poet, Francis Thompson, the author of the most famous cricket poem in the language.

It was intended by his family that he should go on to Oxford to complete his education, and he would have been quite content to go there if he could have devoted his whole energies to sport, but when he learned that he would be expected to undertake a course of academic studies, he decided that he could not face the prospect with any degree of equanimity.

Hornby first played for Lancashire in 1867, and he became a regular member of the side two years later. He was a stocky man of immense strength and splendidly equipped for leadership. It was inevitable that when Edmund Rowley resigned the captaincy of the county side in 1880, Hornby should be invited to succeed him. He feared no man, and he had no time for anyone, either in cricket or in any other sport, who was not prepared to give of his best. A stern and unyielding adversary, he was never prepared to admit defeat until the last wicket had fallen, but he was as generous in his acclaim of a worthy victor as in his praise of a defeated foe. Above all, he had a complete understanding of each of his players, and he won and retained their admiration and respect by his unceasing concern for their welfare – the outstanding characteristic of a great leader.

Hornby was an all-round sportsman if ever there was one. He was always prepared to try his hand at any sport and he was proficient in a great many. He played rugger nine times for England and soccer for Blackburn Rovers; he was a first-class athlete, andaccomplished horseman and a pugnacious boxer, despite his lack of inches, who would issue challenges to professionals for the fun and exhilaration of a fight. Obstreperous spectators at Lancashire's matches were given no quarter by 'Monkey' Hornby. It is recorded that in 1878 when Gloucestershire visited Old Trafford and included in their side the three Grace brothers, the event proved so great an attraction that the accommodation was insufficient for the vast crowd that turned up to watch the cricket. On the Saturday there were 17,000 people on the ground, and drays and lorries were placed behind the ring of seats to serve as temporary stands. Unfortunately a number of spectators, dissatisfied with the makeshift seating, started a riot and began to take up and throw divots of the sacred turf. These acts of sacrilege were too much for Hornby, who exacted swift and summary retribution on one particularly militant demonstrator, dealing him 'a number of hard knocks' and hurling him into the arms of a nearby policeman.

Such incidents were, however, the exception rather than the rule. The setting was peaceful, not violent. Though only three miles from the rapidly expanding city of Manchester, the Old Trafford of those days stood close to the great estate of the de Traffords, the family from whom it acquired its name. At that time deer roamed free in their woodlands and through their green fields. The land which then formed part of their fair estate is now given over to the factories and workshops of the large industrial area of Trafford Park. But in the early days of Lancashire cricket and 'Monkey' Hornby, people could watch the play at Old Trafford and quite easily forget that they were so close to the hustle and bustle of commercial Manchester.

Not a quarter of a mile away, close to the site of the present Manchester United football ground, John Dalton, the famous chemist and the first man to conceive the atomic theory of matter, had been in the habit of spending some of his leisure time playing bowls, and perhaps nearby he had collected in jars from the ponds the specimens of marsh-gas which he needed for his experiments. Those spectators who travelled to the ground by carriage or on horseback would use Stretford Road or the Chester Road, and for those who came by train and alighted at Warwick Road station, there was a path through the fields.

Hornby was a highly individual product of his age, and a leader almost by Divine Right. He lived in a Lancashire which was fast developing into a county of tremendous wealth, and at the other extreme, of terrible poverty. His uncompromising resolution and utter fearlessness ensured his coming to terms with both, and Lancashire cricket was the richer and nobler for his influence and his example.

Though he was one of the most consistently fast scorers in the history of cricket, it would be quite wrong to categorize Hornby as a mere hitter. He was a strong forward player, aggressive from the very first ball he received and he could not abide the idea of the ball dominating the bat – at least while he was batting. He was well aware that his anxiety to score runs quickly was frequently a cause of his getting out, and he would often say to his partner Barlow that he wished he had some of Barlow's patience. The faithful Barlow would reply, with a wry smile, that for his part, he wished he had some of his captain's powers of punishment. Yet the dour patience of Barlow would have been as utterly foreign to Hornby's nature as Hornby's aggression would have been to Barlow's. Together they formed a formidable opening partnership, as respected as it was feared in the county cricket of their time. As a pair they laid the foundations of innings on which their successors could build, Barlow by stern, implacable defence, Hornby by pugnacious, exhilarating attack.

Hornby's partiality for the short, sharp single not infrequently found poor Barlow stranded yards from his crease when the bails were whipped off before his straining limbs and groping bat could attain the haven where they would be. Barlow's often justifiable annoyance was subsequently mollified by the consoling arm of his captain about his shoulders, and the balm of a bright golden sovereign thrust into his honest palm. For such typical sympathy and thoughtfulness was 'Monkey' Hornby respected by his men.

He drove them hard – there could be no denying that. He was a man who knew what he wanted and how to get the results he desired. A stickler for discipline always, he was subtle in its exercise, but he was forthright in expressing his opinions and blunt were the words he used to do so. Woe betide any player who was sluggish in the field whilst Hornby was captain. He set a fine example, never allowed evidence of fatigue to show in his demeanour and expected a similar spartan attitude from his players. The tale is told at Old Trafford of a certain professional who, in an unguarded moment at the end of a hard day's play, remarked to his captain that he felt tired. The next morning he found himself positioned in the deep where he was not normally accustomed to field, and after some hectic scurrying to and fro along the boundary, he was asked by Hornby if he had worked the tiredness out of his system. From that day forward the word was not used in the captain's presence.

Hornby's control on the field was absolute, and he would tolerate no suggestion that was calculated to interfere with his power of decision. When the young Archie MacLaren came fresh from Harrow to play for Lancashire and had the temerity to mention that he would field anywhere except point, it was at point that he was stationed. W.B.Stoddart asked not to be sent into the long field, but into the long field he went.

During Hornby's captaincy the Lancashire fielding became a criterion of excellence. As in all else with which Hornby was connected the keynote was aggression. He was forever seeking a batsman's weakness and once he discovered it, he saw that his bowlers fed it until a crucial mistake delivered the wicket into their hands. His enthusiasm for cricket was immense and vital and he had the inestimable quality of inspiring enthusiasm in others. He studied *Wisden* voraciously and wherever he travelled he carried a copy in his bag. William Howard, a long and devoted servant of Lancashire cricket and cricketers who wrote a most interesting and entertaining book about Old Trafford life behind the scenes and called it 'Fifty Years' Cricket Reminiscences of a non-Player', told how, on one occasion Hornby went off on a holiday to the north of Scotland with his family, leaving him strict instructions to telegraph Lancashire's match scores twice a day and to write him a full report each evening. Press cuttings were also to be forwarded as they became available. The holiday had been arranged to last three weeks, but at the end of the first week, after Hornby had been advised that an old friend was to play, he returned to Old Trafford, scoffing at the 600-odd miles he would have covered before he saw his family again. What Mrs Hornby and the family thought is not recorded, but it would appear that such events were considered of normal occurrence in the domestic life of 'Monkey' Hornby.

Hornby captained the Lancashire side for twelve seasons from 1880 to 1891. He was elected to share the captaincy in 1892 and 1893 with S.M. Crosfield, though he had advised the Committee that he would be unable to turn out regularly. In point of fact he played only four times in each season and the burden of leadership was sustained mainly by Crosfield. For three seasons, from 1894 to 1896, A.C. MacLaren took over the captaincy, but he, too, found it increasingly difficult to turn out regularly and the performance of the side suffered through lack of continuity. Hornby was persuaded to accept the captaincy again in 1897, and he returned to lead the side with all his old vigour and enthusiasm, but he had passed his half-century in years, and at the end of the 1898 season he told the Committee it was time that they found a younger man.

During his years as a player Hornby scored nearly 11,000 runs for Lancashire county. He hit sixteen centuries, his highest score 188 against Derbyshire at Old Trafford in 1881. He must have relished the Derbyshire bowlers that year, for in the return match at Derby he hit them for another 145. In that same game the faithful Barlow performed prodigiously with the ball and took 6 wickets for only 3 runs.

Hornby played for England both at home and in Australia, and though his Test record as a batsman is unimpressive, his appearances were marked by two characteristic displays of courage. He played for M.C.C. in the notable match in 1878 when the Australians won in a day. In the second innings he was hit by the mighty Spofforth, of whom it was said by batsmen who faced him, that he bowled with the speed of light. Most men who had suffered pain at Spofforth's hands would have thought twice about resuming their innings – and decided to stay in the pavilion. Not Hornby. His side was faring so badly that his services were needed. He went out to face the Demon again, and though he could not stem the tide of Australian victory, it was the attitude, so typical of the man, that won the admiration of the spectators.

In Australia in 1879 the crowd swarmed on to the field, following a disputed run-out decision against W.L. Murdoch.

Lord Harris, the England captain was struck by an incensed spectator and for a time it seemed that the English players were in some danger of physical assault. Hornby took control unflinchingly. Though he had been struck in the face himself and his shirt had been half torn from his back, he seized the ringleader by the scruff of the neck and hauled him off into the pavilion and the custody of the law.

In 1882 Hornby captained England in a tremendous match at the Oval when Australia won by seven runs. Hornby and W.G. Grace were always stern opponents and when their paths crossed it was a foregone conclusion that sparks would fly. It is related that on one occasion Hornby attempted to steal a march on the Doctor by unobtrusively altering his field behind W.G. Grace's back, after he had taken guard. The Doctor who was not backward himself when it came to a bit of artful dodging did not much care for doses of his own medicine. One had to be up early in the morning to have any hope of catching him napping, and even then, the odds would be on W.G. to have the last laugh. So it transpired that Hornby's unobtrusive signs to his fieldsmen had not been unobtrusive enough to escape the Doctor's sharp eye.

'I can see ye, Monkey,' W.G. shouted in his high-pitched, squeaky voice. 'I can see what ye're at!'

When his playing days were done, Hornby was by no means lost to Lancashire cricket. He was President of the County Club from 1894 to 1916, and when he died full of years in 1925, he was still taking the keenest interest in the affairs of his beloved Lancashire.

Of all the anecdotes of this early giant of Lancashire cricket I like best one which ascribes to George Yates, another Lancashire player of the 'eighties and early nineties, the desire to emulate the craft of Barlow as a run-stealer in his captain's estimation. On this occasion Yates, at the non-striker's end was batting with Hornby, but he had not been a member of the Lancashire side long enough to be fully conversant with his captain's methods. He knew all about Hornby's liking for the short single, however, and at all costs he was determined not to be found wanting. Hardly had the ball left the bowler's hand when Yates went charging down the pitch, head down. Hornby merely played the ball carefully down into his block-hole, and looking the discomfited Yates squarely in the eye at a distance that could only be measured in inches, he enquired testily, 'What the hell are you doing here, Yates?'

Richard Gorton Barlow, for ever linked with Hornby in Francis Thompson's poem was a Bolton man, born at Barrow Bridge in 1850. Like Hornby he was a cricket enthusiast, but unlike his future captain, he learned his craft the hard way. In his schooldays he used to practise with a crude bat, hewn from a rough piece of wood and a ball pieced together with cloth and string. In his reminiscences he told how he would play truant from school and his methods of obtaining proficiency as a cricketer were thorough and workmanlike, two qualities he was to exhibit throughout his life.

Barlow had a fetish for keeping himself in perfect physical condition and he was supremely confident of his own abilities, especially as far as his cricket was concerned. Up to the age of sixty-four, at which time most of us would be content to relax in carpet slippers in an armchair by the fireside, he was willing to take on, single wicket, any man in England of his own age.

Barlow was as cautious as Hornby was aggressive, but he was never negative. As a boy he had batted and bowled left-handed, but on the advice of his father he started to bat right-handed to avoid the appearance of awkwardness and stiffness of left-handed batsmen which the elder Barlow could not abide. He used mainly the forward defensive stroke, and though over the years he acquired the reputation of a stone-waller of the breed of Scotton, Louis Hall and Alec Bannerman, it is interesting to note that his contemporaries never referred to him as a slow player. The rough wickets of Barlow's day favoured the bowlers, and it was often a considerable achievement for a batsman to keep his wicket at all. The long innings he played in match after match against some of the best bowling in England were a measure of his technical ability and the efficacy of his self-training.

On numerous occasions Barlow saved Lancashire from defeat by his resolute defence. Twelve times he carried his bat through an innings, and on many more occasions his was the last wicket to fall. He scored well over 7,000 runs for the county in an age when comparatively few matches were played, and his batting average (20) was only 3 runs less than Hornby's.

Unfortunately Old Trafford did not see what is generally reckoned to have been Barlow's finest innings. It was played at Trent Bridge for the North of England against the Australian team of 1884. The North scored 91 (Barlow not out 10) in their first innings and the Australians replied with 100.

Spofforth who had found the wicket in the first innings immensely to his liking prophesied jubilantly that the Englishmen wouldn't make 60 in their second knock, and when he had shot out Shrewsbury, Scotton, Barnes, Gunn and Bates for 53 runs it seemed that his estimate might not be far wrong. Then Flowers joined Barlow, and the pair added 158 for the sixth wicket. Barlow was last out after scoring 101 without offering a chance in four and a half hours. He completed a remarkable all-round performance by taking 10 wickets for 45 in the two Australian innings.

Another noteworthy performance took place at Trent Bridge. In 1881 he carried his bat through a Lancashire innings which yielded 69 runs of which Barlow in 2½ hours claimed only five! A fortnight later in the return match at Liverpool he again carried his bat through Lancashire's first innings, scoring 44 out of 93. In the second innings he narrowly missed the distinction of remaining on the field for the whole of the match when he was next to last out for 49 in a total of 188.

Barlow's bowling was more than useful, and he was one of the first cricketers to bat right-handed and bowl left. For Lancashire he took 726 wickets at just over 13 runs apiece. He was closer to medium pace than slow, tidily accurate, and he could spin the ball away from the bat. He also used the left-hander's ball that goes with the bowler's arm, and it was said that he had a special ball which he reserved exclusively for W.G.Grace. The story is probably apocryphal, but it was a fact that no other bowler of his time had such a successful record in dismissing the Doctor cheaply. In the Gentlemen v Players match at the Oval in 1884, he performed a notable 'hat-trick', dismissing W.G. with the last ball of one over and off the first two balls of the next, having Shuter and Read caught at the wicket.

In the Oval Test Match of 1882, when A.N. Hornby captained the England side, Barlow took 5 Australian wickets for 19 runs, and in 1887, again for the Players against the Gentlemen he skimmed the cream from the amateur batting with the wickets of W.G., Alfred Lyttelton, Hornby, A.P. Lucas, A.G. Steel, A.H. Trevor and A.H. Evans for 55 runs.

His all-round ability can be gauged from his record against Australia. He played in 17 Test matches, twelve of them in

succession, scoring 591 runs and taking 35 wickets. He toured
Australia three times, and to this day Barlow is the only cricketer
to be picked for England with the specific intention that he
should open both the batting and the bowling. On these three
tours he did not miss a single match.

Barlow was a sharp and vigilant fieldsman, usually at point
where every batsman was soon made aware of his presence.
Apart from his cricket he was a useful goalkeeper at soccer, and
he achieved further distinction both as a referee (he had charge of
a famous cup-tie when Preston North End scored 26 goals
against Hyde United without reply) and as a first-class umpire
when his playing days were done.

For some years Barlow kept a shop in Stretford Road, a short
distance from the Old Trafford ground and there printed songs
in praise of Lancashire cricket could be purchased or ordered by
post by enclosing nine penny stamps. He fancied himself as
something of an inventor, and when the Old Trafford Test
match of 1890 was rained off, without a ball having been bowled,
he observed that much of the disappointment could have been
avoided if only his patent wicket-protector had been brought
into use.

When he finally retired Barlow took himself off to the coast at
Lytham where he packed his home with trophies and mementoes
of his cricket, even to the extent of having a stained-glass
window with himself as the main figure. There were cricket
pictures in the tiles of his fireplace and bats in every room, even in
the bathroom to remind this true professional and loyal son of
Lancashire of his happy days in the sun.

To the Old Trafford crowd of the 'seventies and 'eighties the
sight of Hornby and Barlow walking from the pavilion to the
wicket to initiate a Lancashire innings brought feelings of
pleasant satisfaction. God was in his Heaven and all was well
with the world. They were a splendid looking pair, strength and
physical fitness inherent in their every movement. In appearance
they were markedly contrasted – Hornby small, fair, hair parted
straight down the middle with a small military moustache,
invariably bare-headed; Barlow dark, thick-set, his full moustache curling down to his beard. Hornby swung his bat jauntily, a
knight of the ancient order scenting a battle to be fought; Barlow,
less flamboyant of movement and gesture, the work- man with a
formidable job to tackle. If Hornby was the Squire of Lancashire

cricket, Barlow was the honest yeoman, but a yeoman with a craftsman's eye and sensibilities. So the battle would be joined and the run stealing would begin. Years later, on a visit to Lord's when his own red roses came down from the north, Francis Thompson would recall nostalgically his Hornby and his Barlow, the heroes of his young manhood and the blissful days when he could escape from the drudgery of his medical studies to the bright sunlight of Old Trafford. The poem 'At Lord's' is of four stanzas, the first stanza repeated at the end. The two middle stanzas are not of particularly distinguished verse; some of the rhymes are clumsy and the scansion is occasionally awry, but in the stanza that has found its way deservedly into anthologies Thompson uses Hornby and Barlow to symbolize his longing in middle-age to turn time back to the happier, less complicated days of his youth:-

'It is little I repair to matches of the Southron folk,
Though my own red roses there may blow;
It is little I repair to matches of the Southron folk,
Though the red roses crest the caps, I know.
For the field is full of shades as I near the shadowy coast,
And a ghostly batsman plays to the bowling of a ghost,
And I look through my tears on a soundless clapping host,
As the run-stealers flicker to and fro,
    To and fro:-
O my Hornby and my Barlow long ago!'

Apart from their secure place in Lancashire cricket history and records, Hornby and Barlow are remembered at Old Trafford by two roads of faded Edwardian red-brick houses, lying between the ground and the main Chester Road. It is safe to say that few if any of the people who live in those houses, know who Hornby and Barlow were. Their successors, MacLaren, Duckworth, Washbrook and Statham now have glass and concrete palaces named after them, modern architectural masterpieces which tower high over the field where they played their cricket. Hornby and Barlow trod that same rich turf when the Lancashire County Club was young, and though their deeds may not be so readily called to mind, they, too, were giants in their day.

III

Alec Watson

Alec Watson was another giant of Lancashire's early days. He was a Scotsman who was first noticed by the Rusholme Club whilst he was touring with a team from Lanarkshire. He seems to have been something of a cricket mercenary, playing in his younger days for any side which was prepared to pay him an honest penny, and his services were sought alike by touring teams and by local sides who were matched against them. Such was his involvement in games of cricket at this period of his life that one need not have been surprised to find Watson's name appearing in both teams in the same match! I have been unable to trace any specific instance, but that is not to say that the phenomenon never occurred.

After a spell with the Manchester Club Watson was promoted to the county side in 1871, when at the age of 27 he gained a place because of the absence of a wicket-keeper. Evidently he was prepared to try his hand at anything, but at that time his speciality was fast round-arm bowling. Ultimately he abandoned fast bowling for off-breaks which he bowled with such telling accuracy that he was capable of shutting up one end almost indefinitely. He took many wickets with his most dangerous ball that kept very low after pitching, so many wickets, in fact, that one doubts the strict accuracy of a contemporary who wrote that 'Watson's slows crept gently up to the wicket'.

In the twenty-two years spanned by Watson's first-class career he took 1279 wickets for Lancashire at 13.47 runs each, a record that makes him one of the most successful and dependable bowlers in the county's cricket history. It is all the more remarkable when one considers that in Watson's day fixtures were fewer and farther between than they are today.

Watson's earliest games for the county were played under Edmund Rowley's captaincy. In 1873 he and McIntyre must have been rated the scourge of Surrey, for they bowled unchanged through both matches. At Old Trafford Surrey were put out for 44 and 105, and in the return game at the Oval, Surrey's total of 33 still remains their lowest score ever against Lancashire.

In 1876 the two bowlers repeated their performance in the two matches against Derbyshire, and so comprehensively did they monopolize the Lancashire bowling that year that they shared 140 of the 171 wickets.

Watson played a considerable part in Lancashire's sharing of the Championship with Notts in 1879, and in 1880, the first season of A.N.Hornby's captaincy, he took 79 wickets, more than in any season to that date.

In 1881, Lancashire, unbeaten in thirteen county games, won the Championship outright for the first time, *Wisden* hailing the record as 'a series of brilliant successes almost unparalleled in the history of county cricket'. It is claimed with some justification that this Championship-winning team was the strongest fielding side in Lancashire's history, and Watson played his part in the slips as well as with the ball.

The bowling could be said to have lacked variety, for Watson, Barlow, Nash and Steel were all under medium pace, but, as *Lillywhite's Annual* pointed out, it seemed to matter little who went on to bowl first; the result was always satisfactory.

Lancashire and Notts again shared the Championship in 1882. Cambridge University came to Old Trafford in June, straight from a notable victory over the Australians, and were welcomed by a fall of snow. Watson and Barlow capitalized on this frigid reception by putting the University out for 31, and in subsequent matches they shot out Kent for 71 and 139 and Derbyshire for 77 and 55.

Though a slow bowler, Alec Watson was not exempt from accusations of throwing, which at this time were also being directed against his Lancashire colleagues, Crossland and Nash. It is said that those who were of the opinion that Watson threw, supported their argument by pointing out how well he could control his length against the wind. This seems curious logic, to say the least, and it cannot have been taken very seriously by Lord Harris, who in 1885 objected to the inclusion of Crossland and Nash in the Lancashire team to play Kent, but did not embrace Watson in his objection.

In 1886 Watson distinguished himself at Lord's when Lancashire defeated M.C.C. in one day. M.C.C. were put out for 30 in their first innings, and he took 6 wickets for 8 runs in 15 overs.

In the following season, an exceptionally dry summer, Watson took a hundred wickets on pitches all in favour of batsmen and was rated, with Attewell and Lohmann one of the three best bowlers in the country.

At the age of 45 in 1889, he could be reckoned a veteran, but his bowling certainly gave no indication that he had reached the sere and yellow stage. He took 90 wickets that summer at 12.65 runs each, and finished fourth in the national averages, immediately behind his county colleagues, Briggs and Mold.

With Johnny Briggs Watson formed a formidable combination. Possibly their finest performance together was against Sussex in 1890, when they bowled unchanged through the two innings and finished with these remarkable figures –

	1st Innings				2nd Innings			
	Q.	M.	R.	W.	O.	M.	R.	W.
Watson	27	21	7	5	19.4	16	6	4
Briggs	27	18	25	5	19	11	16	5

The sands of Watson's long career were running out, however. He broke down with a strain in the summer of 1891, and though he returned to the side in the following season, and with Briggs and Mold bore the brunt of the bowling, he dropped out of the team in 1893.

Five years later, when he was 54 years of age, the Lancashire Committee, alarmed at the deterioration in bowling strength, asked him to hold himself in readiness to play against Surrey at the Oval. Watson wisely declined. He had been too good a professional not to realize that, after five years away from the first-class game, he could never again recapture the form of his greatest days. His sagacity in turning down the Committee's behest was conspicuously demonstrated when Surrey ran up a score of 634 and Tom Hayward helped himself to a treble hundred.

The photographs of the Championship-winning Lancashire teams of 1879 and 1881 show Watson as a man of rather melancholy features. I imagine that he took his cricket seriously, for it was his livelihood, and earning a living is a serious enough business. The walrus moustache of the 1879 photograph has been neatly trimmed in 1881 to almost a replica of A.N. Hornby's.

Over his cricket flannels Watson is wearing a formal jacket and waistcoat. A heavy watch-chain, dangling from his waistcoat pockets is the emblem of late Victorian commercial respectability.

The earlier photograph stamps Watson clearly as a professional: in the later photograph he could quite easily be taken for one of the amateurs, were it not for the fact that he is standing, and the amateurs have been provided with chairs.

There is a clue here, I fancy, to Watson's character and outlook. He was not consciously aping his superiors in that 1881 print. He was a professional cricketer, a craftsman, and as an honest practitioner of his craft he considered himself the equal of any of them.

Alec Watson practised his craft in the formative years of Lancashire cricket and helped significantly to lay the foundation on which successive generations of cricketers have built. For that and for the fine bowler he was, he will always be remembered.

IV

Arthur Mold

Arthur Mold first played for Lancashire in 1889 when Alec Watson's career had entered its twilight zone.

Mold was a Northamptonshire man, born near Banbury, and he played a few games for his native county before moving to Lancashire. In his first season at Old Trafford he quickly made his mark as one of the fastest bowlers in the country. He took 13 Yorkshire wickets for 111 runs at Huddersfield and finished third in the national bowling averages with 102 wickets at 11.83.

There seems little doubt that he occasionally 'threw'. Harry Makepeace would recall in later years that, as a boy, he had seen Mold bowl at Aigburth, and players and spectators alike were convinced that his action sometimes transgressed the rules.

In those early days, however, suspicions of 'throwing' had not assumed the serious proportions they reached by the turn of the century, and the controversy that was to envelop Mold and ultimately end his career was still far away in the future.

In 1890 Mold again took over a hundred wickets, and endeared himself further to Lancastrian hearts with two notable performances against Yorkshire, taking 9 wickets for 40 at Old Trafford and 13 for 76 in a big Lancashire victory at Huddersfield. *Wisden's* rapture, however, was modified and it was moved to remark that it hoped 'Mold will make efforts to keep his action above the breath of suspicion'.

W.G. Grace seemed to have no such doubts and he pronounced Mold 'the fairest of fast bowlers'. Mold celebrated the good Doctor's endorsement of his action by taking 129 wickets in the following season at 12.62 runs apiece. In the two Somerset games he had 26 wickets at a total cost of 240 runs, and against both Gloucester and Sussex 20 wickets in the home and away engagements.

Mold was a man of commanding physique, with powerful shoulders and standing over six feet in height. He was genuinely fast, though he took a run of only seven paces, and on any type of wicket he posed problems for the best batsman. On a wicket less than perfect he could be an absolute terror and his breakback was as deadly as a cobra's sting.

In 1892 he was chosen as one of *Wisden*'s Five Cricketers of the Year. Again he took over a hundred wickets, thirteen of them against Middlesex when he hit the stumps ten times. When Somerset came to Old Trafford and were beaten in a day Mold took 8 for 40 and after rain at Tonbridge he made the ball fly so devastatingly that he had second innings figures of 9 for 29 and a match analysis of 13 for 91. He bettered this performance at Brighton taking 14 Sussex wickets in one day for 159 runs.

In the summer of 1893 Mold took 142 wickets in Lancashire's matches at slightly over 15 runs each. Five times that season he took eight wickets in an innings and he was chosen to play for England in three Tests against Australia, displacing the great Tom Richardson of Surrey. Sadly he failed to do himself full justice; his 7 wickets cost over 33 runs each.

The seasons of 1894 and 1895 were Mold's most successful summers in first-class cricket. In each he took over 200 wickets in all matches. In Championship matches alone in 1894 his 144 wickets cost only 11 runs apiece. Somerset were again beaten in a day and Mold was the main scourge, taking 13 wickets for 60 runs. His 7 for 10 in the first innings included a 'hat trick' and ten balls later three wickets in four balls.

Sussex once more felt the searing fire of his bowling; at Old Trafford he took seven of their second innings wickets for 17 runs and at Brighton he had a match analysis of 15 for 87. In three successive matches he claimed 33 wickets, twenty-seven of them clean bowled. He had thirteen against Gloucestershire, though Johnny Briggs deprived him of W.G.'s wicket in both innings, and another thirteen against Kent.

In the wonderful summer of 1895 when Grace scored his thousand runs in May and hit his hundredth century, when Archie MacLaren set up a new individual scoring record with his 424 at Taunton and batsmen revelled in the sun, Mold helped to restore the balance between bat and ball and materially assisted Lancashire to second place in the Championship by taking 182 wickets in county matches alone at 13 runs each.

He had 16 for 111 against Kent at Old Trafford, 15 for 85 against Notts at Trent Bridge (including a spell of 4 wickets in four balls) and 11 Yorkshire wickets for 128 at Sheffield. Rather more surprisingly he distinguished himself as a batsman by helping Albert Ward to put on 111 for the last wicket in the Leicestershire match at Old Trafford. It is said that no one was more astonished at this performance than Arthur Mold himself.

He was handicapped by a hand injury in 1896 which caused him some discomfort, but Mold was made of spartan stuff and he continued to bowl even whilst undergoing treatment. It argues well for his wonderful spirit that he could still take 137 wickets, though the cost (17.62) was higher than in previous summers.

In the match against Surrey at the Oval which attracted considerable interest as a measurement of Mold's prowess against that of Tom Richardson, Mold, according to a contemporary newspaper account, sent one of Lohmann's bails 63 yards 6 inches in the direction of square leg. I relish the thought of the distance being checked. Was it a challenge to Tom Richardson to better the feat if he could? If the bail did move so far in the direction of square leg, it must have provided an astonishing example of Mold's devastating break-back!

Injuries plagued him again in the summers of 1897 and 1898 and he was absent from several matches. In 1897 he failed for the first time in seven seasons to take his hundred wickets, though he was only two short and finished eighth in the national averages.

He was back to the hundred, however, in 1899, when due to the breakdowns of Hallam and Briggs, he bore the brunt of the Lancashire bowling, but his 115 wickets cost over 18 runs each and his figures reflected the increased amount of work he had been obliged to undertake.

In 1900 he had a much better season, and though he just failed to take his hundred wickets, he finished second in the averages to Wilfred Rhodes with 97 at 14 apiece. He plundered the Sussex batting at Hastings to take 12 for 46, but the first signs of the trouble that was to end his career appeared at Trent Bridge in June. He was no-balled for 'throwing' by the Australian umpire, Phillips and he bowled only one more over in that game.

Mold continued to play for the remainder of the season, though he did not take part in his own benefit match against Yorkshire. Whatever the rights or wrongs of his action, it had become increasingly evident that the deliveries of too many bowlers were tinged with suspicion.

Phillips, who had previously no-balled the formidable Ernest Jones in Australia, also 'called' C. B. Fry of Sussex and Tyler of

Somerset that season, and during the winter the county captains
met to consider the whole question of unfair bowling.

Mold was one of several bowlers the county captains at this
meeting agreed not to use, but the Lancashire Committee,
standing on its dignity, decided to ignore the agreement and
questioned the right of the county captains to make it.
Unfortunately Mold again fell foul of Umpire Phillips in the
Somerset match at Old Trafford. He was no-balled no less than
eighteen times. Police protection was required for Phillips as he
left the ground, but the damage was done. Many of Mold's
contemporaries were still convinced that his action was basically
fair and a film taken of it in the nets at Lord's was said to reveal no
suggestion of throwing.

Poor Mold bore himself with considerable dignity throughout
the unfortunate controversy. There was much sympathy for his
view that if there were any doubt about the legality of his action,
he should have been stopped at the beginning of his career, since
to label him a thrower at the end of it, inevitably detracted from
the merit of his performances.

That these performances were great cannot be denied. For
Lancashire alone in his twelve seasons he took 1541 wickets at
slightly over 15 runs each in 259 matches. His average of nearly
six wickets a match has not been bettered by any of the great
Lancashire bowlers; it is almost two more than either Johnny
Briggs, his wonderful little contemporary or Brian Statham of
more recent times.

Thirty-six times with Johnny Briggs at the other end, he
bowled unchanged through an innings, and if he never sustained
the brilliance of Lockwood nor the power of Tom Richardson, at
his best he was the equal of both these great bowlers.

That, I fancy, is how Arthur Mold would have liked to be
remembered.

V

Johnny Briggs

Johnny Briggs, a lovable and cheery cricketer, was the idol of the Old Trafford crowds in the days when he played for Lancashire county.

By birth he was a Nottinghamshire man, and he first played for Lancashire in 1879 when he was only seventeen years of age. In his early days at Old Trafford he appears to have gained a place in the county side on his fielding ability alone, for his batting and bowling figures were not sufficiently impressive to set the cricket world afire. Yet 'Monkey' Hornby must have recognized in the cheerful, good-humoured little man a potential cricketer and there is no doubt that a player with as sunny a disposition as that of Johnny Briggs is an asset to any cricket dressing room.

Briggs was a busy cricketer, always eager to be in the game and seemingly tireless. He loved his cricket and he possessed the happy quality of being able to communicate his good humour and enthusiasm both to the players and the spectators. He originally came to Old Trafford as a batsman, and his batting, once he had settled down, was good enough to win him a place in most county sides. For so small a man he could hit the ball with the most incredible power. He was particularly partial to the offside slash, a stroke something between a cut and a drive, played as the ball was rising.

As he developed his bowling his batting became more reckless, and his impatience, often a useful asset as a bowler, but a frequent source of error in a batsman, cost him his wicket on many occasions when greater caution could have brought him a lot more runs.

His bowling improved when he decreased his pace to slow medium, but probably the main reason for Briggs's development as a bowler was the increase in the amount of bowling he was asked to undertake when Crossland was disqualified from playing for Lancashire on a residential irregularity. Briggs had no such difficulty. Though he had been born in Nottingham, his family had moved to Lancashire whilst Johnny was still a child and he was to spend the rest of his life in the county.

Briggs was a left-arm bowler with almost an apology of a run – a mere couple of paces, but he had an extensive repertoire of deliveries with which to tax and confound the batsman, and he exploited them with consummate cunning. The great C.B. Fry once described him as 'a professor of diddling, considered as one of the exact sciences'. His diddling embraced subtle variations of spin, length, flight and pace, and he was apt on occasions to unleash a fast, straight ball, well disguised and quite unexpected. He was a brilliant fielder to his own bowling, moving alertly to the off- or leg-side to intercept a drive, and walking quickly back to his mark to continue his over. No bowler got through an over quicker than Johnny Briggs. He allowed batsmen no pause for relaxation or respite.

Briggs was as alert in mind as in his movements and many a batsman was deluded by his happy banter and chatter into thinking that he lacked seriousness and application. They could not have been more mistaken. He was in business to get them out in the shortest possible time, and all his energies and cunning were directed towards this end. To quote C.B.Fry again, 'He beams upon you before and after your innings. The shorter your innings, the happier he is towards you. He passes you a cheery time of day. He enquires with feeling after your health and form. He rubs the ball in the dust, takes two steps and serves you a fast yorker instead of the high-tossed slow you expected. You retire. He smiles. What could be pleasanter?'

What, indeed? Charles Fry, who was an excellent judge of a cricketer, considered Briggs more resourceful, if less accurate than Bobby Peel, the Yorkshire bowler, the other outstanding left-hander of his time.

The sharpness of his fielding became a byword on the cricket fields of England. His short, rotund figure and agility gave him the appearance of a bouncing rubber ball, but for all his chubbiness, he had a speed which put him at cover not far below the class of his Lancashire colleague, the formidable Vernon Royle.

Briggs's love of cricket was equalled only by his enjoyment of the company of the men who played it. He was ready for a game anytime and anywhere and often he would stop on his way to or from Old Trafford to join in a scratch game with a group of youngsters. Children particularly loved him, for he could talk to them and share their games as an equal.

Briggs took 1688 wickets for Lancashire for 15.65 runs apiece, and scored over 10,000 runs in his twenty seasons of first-class cricket. He is, in fact, the only Lancashire player to have scored 10,000 runs and taken over 1,000 wickets for the county and his tally of wickets has been bettered only by Brian Statham.

'Roses' matches brought the best out of Johnny Briggs. In 1891 after he had bowled Yorkshire to defeat at Bradford, he gave their batsmen another dose of the same medicine in the return game at Old Trafford, taking 6 wickets for 76 in the first. innings and 8 for 46 in the second. He opened the Lancashire bowling in both innings. No nonsense in those days about reserving the new ball exclusively for the faster bowlers!

Yorkshire won the first of the two annual arguments in 1892 – by four wickets after a close struggle. Peel for Yorkshire and Briggs for Lancashire each took a good haul of wickets in a low-scoring game. A young man from Kirkheaton by the name of George Herbert Hirst, who was to cause Lancashire a heap of trouble in the years ahead made his 'roses' début in this game and took 4 wickets for 32 in Lancashire's second innings.

Lancashire exacted sweet revenge for this reverse at Old Trafford where they scored one of their most convincing wins of the season by an innings and 83 runs. Johnny Briggs had the sort of match every cricketer must dream about. He scored 115 runs with the bat, bowled unchanged through Yorkshire's first innings, taking 8 wickets for 113 runs in just under 50 overs, and with Alec Watson as his accomplice again demolished their batting in the second.

At Headingley in 1893, in another low-scoring match, Briggs steered Lancashire to an innings victory with a devastating spell in Yorkshire's second innings, when he took 8 of their wickets for only 19 runs.

The August game at Old Trafford in the same season brought one of the closest and tensest finishes ever associated with 'roses' cricket. Though rain interfered with play a large crowd attended the match. The two sides made only 223 runs between them in the four completed innings. Lancashire were put out for 64 in their first innings, but Yorkshire could make only 58 in reply. In their second innings Lancashire added another 50, and Yorkshire were left with a mere 57 to get to win.

Twenty-four of those runs had been scored before the first wicket fell, and there must have been very few people in that Old Trafford crowd who would have been prepared to bet on a Lancashire victory. Then wickets began to tumble, until at the fall of the ninth only six more runs were needed. George Ulyett, known as 'Happy Jack' because of his incessant whistle, a kindly man who had given his bat to a blind boy in the corresponding match the previous season, faced Johnny Briggs. The moment was fraught with pregnant possibilities. Briggs knew full well that if he gave 'Happy Jack' a ball to hit, he would hit it, no matter what the state of the game. In fact Ulyett, presented with such a ball, would sense a Yorkshire victory to be achieved by one lusty clout. So Johnny Briggs tossed up the ball for Ulyett to hit. Hit it Ulyett did, and away it soared towards the boundary. But Albert Ward's safe hands were under it as it dropped, and Albert Ward put down very few chances.

Johnny had won his momentous gamble, and the Lancashire players returned triumphant from the field, to the joyful back-slapping of the members and the chortles of glee that yet another of Johnny's artful dodges had come off. Apart from the last stratagem which had given Lancashire the game, Briggs had had a most successful match with 11 wickets for 60 runs.

Sir Neville Cardus has recounted in his essay on Johnny Briggs that amidst all the jubilation in the Lancashire dressing room, the little man sat with ashen face. Though his little dodge had been worked so successfully, his heart, according to Cardus, had well nigh burst with apprehension at the thought of the risk he had taken. George Ulyett's thoughts were not recorded, but such was the pleasantness of his disposition that one cannot imagine regret or depression remaining with him for very long.

A particularly successful season in 1888 won for Briggs inclusion in *Wisden*'s gallery of 'Six Great Bowlers', introduced that year for the first time. He was in good company, for his companions were Lohmann, Peel, S.M.J. Woods, Ferris and Turner. In that season he topped the bowling averages with 160 wickets, and scored over 800 runs. Against Derbyshire he had the remarkable match record of 13 wickets for 39 runs, he had another 13 in the Middlesex match, 12 against Gloucester and 13 again at the end of the season against the touring Australians at Scarborough.

Briggs played 33 times for England – thirty-one times against

Australia and twice against South Africa. In all he took 118 wickets at an average of 17.74 and scored over 800 runs (average 18). He toured South Africa in the winter of 1888, in one Test taking 6 wickets for 73 runs, and then at Cape Town 15 wickets (fourteen clean bowled) for 28 runs. Another of his distinctions, not perhaps generally known, is that he is the only England cricketer to have scored a century and performed the 'hat-trick' against Australia. He hit the top score for England in the Test match at Sydney in 1887, and in recognition of this feat, the Prince of Wales, afterwards King Edward VII, presented him with a gold medal, bearing his initials, set in a pattern of seven diamonds. This was subsequently presented to the Lancashire County Club and is still in its possession.

It was at Sydney in 1894 that he and Peel bowled England to victory in a match that Australia seemed to have safely won. England had been obliged to follow on after a poor first-innings showing, but the batting improved to such an extent in the second innings that Australia were set to score 177 to win. By the evening of the penultimate day they had reached 113 for 2, and few would have prepared for an England victory. However, on a sticky wicket, entirely to their liking, Peel and Briggs shot through the remainder of the batting and England won by ten runs.

After another Test at Lord's in which Arthur Shrewsbury distinguished himself with the bat, and the Lancashire pair Barlow and Briggs performed nobly with the ball, the following piece of doggerel appeared in a London newspaper:-

'Thanks to you, we're dancing jigs,
Shrewsbury, Barlow and Briggs.
Who'll call England's cricket low,
Briggs and Shrewsbury and Barlow.
Here's to your health, ye glorious three!
Barlow, Briggs and Shrewsbury.'

Johnny Briggs deserved better than this, as he deserved a much better benefit than fate (assisted more than a little by a certain Yorkshire captain) provided for him. His benefit year was 1894, when he was still only 32 years of age, though he had been playing with Lancashire for 15 seasons. In appreciation of his wonderful services to the county, he was awarded the 'roses' game at Old Trafford as his benefit match. It was an extraordinary game in every way. Lancashire were captained by A.N. Hornby, who had attained the office of President that year. There were 15,000 spectators present on the first day to pay their tribute to Lancashire's greatest bowler.

The first sensation occurred when Lord Hawke, the Yorkshire captain, objected to the prepared wicket which had been covered for the benefit match, on the grounds that the covering would put too much advantage on winning the toss. During the previous night there had been a storm and the wicket had been protected from the rain. Lord Hawke's objection is difficult to follow, for the alternative was to make ready, with all possible despatch, an unprepared, uncovered wicket which must certainly have been open to the very objection he had made to the original wicket – that it would put too high an advantage on winning the toss.

The large crowd fretted and fumed whilst a new wicket was rolled out. In the event Lancashire won the toss, but Hornby made the wrong decision, electing to bat. Lancashire lost their first four wickets without a run being scored, seven were down for 17, and they were all out for 50. When they replied Yorkshire were rather more successful, but 7 wickets had fallen for 76 runs and there seemed small prospect of a winning lead. Then Moorhouse and Mounsey in an eighth wicket stand and Hunter, the wicket keeper, with a stubborn innings, doubled the score, giving their side a lead of 102 runs.

It was too much for Lancashire. They collapsed again on the second morning, before the bowling of Hirst, Peel and Wainwright and the proceedings were all over before lunch, Yorkshire winning by an innings and 4 runs. Cruel luck for Johnny Briggs who received only about £1,000 as reward for his services to Lancashire and England cricket.

The gods who had endowed him with such rich talent and lovable qualities played a last scurvy trick on poor Briggs. He was attacked by epilepsy during the Leeds Test Match of 1899. He recovered sufficiently to play cricket again the following year, to take his hundred wickets and in the Worcestershire match at Old Trafford to take all ten wickets in an innings for 55 runs. Then the curtain came down on the career of this little man, beloved of the Lancashire crowds. He suffered a relapse which necessitated his confinement in a mental home and he died two years later at the age of 39.

In an age when people's ideas of Heaven are undergoing radical changes, and when even Christian Bishops are telling us that we must not believe literally the conception of a perfect existence beyond this vale of tears, I still like to think that in some Elysian Field, where it is always high summer and where one day we may watch the immortals of cricket in action again, Johnny Briggs, bubbling with infectious laughter and zest for the game, will be taking his two little steps to the wicket and diddling out the best of them as in his great and happy years.

VI

A.C. MacLaren

Archie MacLaren was captain of Lancashire county for three seasons from 1894 to 1896, and again from 1900 to 1907. He was a Manchester man by birth, though his family came originally from Scotland. His father James MacLaren was for many years Treasurer and later President of the County Club. Young Archie spent much time at Old Trafford in his formative years, and he had the benefit of some careful coaching. He was an attentive and diligent learner and he worked hard to perfect his batting.

At Elstree, before going on to Harrow, he was coached by Vernon Royle, one of Lancashire's greatest cover-points, so that when he arrived at Harrow there was already in him considerable natural talent as well as much acquired wisdom. He succeeded F.S. Jackson as captain of cricket at Harrow, after first distinguishing himself by scoring 55 and 67 against Eton when only 15 years of age. In his fourth year (1890) he hit 76 of a total of 133 when only one other boy attained double figures.

Only a month later he played in the county side at Brighton, and after Barlow, Sugg and Albert Ward had been dismissed for 23, he scored 108 in 130 minutes, without giving a chance. Expert judges were impressed not only by the score, but by the manner in which it had been made. A batsman of style and panache had arrived.

In the next season MacLaren played in only five county games, and though he did not score a century, he topped the Lancashire batting averages. In 1892 he scored hundreds against Gloucestershire at Liverpool, and again against Sussex at Brighton, and with two centuries in his first three, many might have been forgiven for thinking that Brighton would become one of his favourite grounds. Curiously enough, he never scored another hundred there.

When S.M. Crosfield, who had been elected captain for the 1894 season, was unable to undertake the duties. MacLaren was appointed to take over. He was then only 22, and though it could

not be said at that time that his batting for the county had as yet
fulfilled the promise of his schooldays and his first century at
Brighton, there could be no doubt that there was cricket enough
in him and a devotion to the game that could only augur well for
the future.

His first two months of captaincy were not to set Old Trafford
ablaze with excitement; the seven fixtures in May and June
produced only one win and six defeats, but there was a
tremendous improvement in the following season when Lancashire finished runners up to Surrey in the Championship, and
MacLaren achieved a personal distinction in the Somerset match
at Taunton which stands as a record to this day.

He had been touring in Australia during the winter, but had
travelled home later than his colleagues and he missed the
opening of the English season. He played in two games without
exciting remark, and after it had been announced that he had
accepted a position as a schoolmaster, he was away from the side
for the next seven matches. He rejoined the team at Taunton, and
though he had not played first-class cricket for five weeks, he
went in first and hit the Somerset bowling for 424 runs in ten
minutes under eight hours. The full score-card is well worthy of
reproduction:-

LANCASHIRE
1st Innings

A.C. MacLaren	c. Fowler	b. Gamlin	424
A. Ward	c. R. Palairet	b. Tyler	64
Paul	c. Gamlin	b. L. Palairet	177
Hallam	c. Fowler	b. L. Palairet	6
C.H. Benton	c & b Fowler		43
Sugg	c. Wickham	b. Woods	41
Tinsley	c. Gamlin	b. Woods	0
Baker	St. Wickham	b. L. Palairet	23
Briggs	NOT OUT		9
Smith	c. Trask	b. L. Palairet	0
Mold	c. R. Palairet	b. Gamlin	0
Extras			14
			801

SOMERSET
1st Innings

L.C.H. Palairet	b. Briggs		30
G. Fowler	c. Sub	b. Hallam	39
R.C.N. Palairet	c. Hallam	b. Mold	2
H.T. Stanley	c. Smith	b. Briggs	8
R.B. Porch	run out		1
S.M.J. Woods	c. Smith	b. Mold	11
J.E. Trask	c Ward	b. Mold	11
A.P. Wickham	b. Mold		3
Tyler	NOT OUT		15
E.W. Bartlett	b. Briggs		4
Gamlin	St. Smith	b Briggs	0
Extras			2
		Total	143

SOMERSET
2nd Innings

L.C.H. Palairet	b. Mold		4
G. Fowler	c. MacLaren	b. Mold	46
R.C.N. Palairet	St. Smith	b. Briggs	7
H.T. Stanley	c. Smith	b. Mold	12
R.B. Porch	c. MacLaren	b. Mold	1
S.M.J. Woods	b. Briggs		55
J.E. Trask	c & b Mold		26
A.P. Wickham	NOT OUT		0
Tyler	b Briggs		41
E.W. Bartlett	c. Mold	b. Briggs	6
Gamlin	Ht Wkt	b Briggs	0
Extras			8
		Total	206

BOWLING ANALYSIS

Lancashire	First Innings			
	O.	M.	R.	W.
Tyler	59	5	212	1
S.M.J. Woods	46	5	163	2
L. Palairet	44	10	133	4
Gamlin	26	8	100	2
G. Fowler	23	5	97	1
R. Palairet	11	3	41	0
J.E. Trask	2	0	9	0
R.B. Porch	5	0	16	0
E.W. Bartlett	6	0	16	0

SOMERSET

	First Innings				Second Innings			
	O.	M.	R.	W.	O.	M.	R.	W.
Briggs	37.3	15	59	4	37	17	78	5
Mold	35	15	75	4	33	11	76	5
Hallam	2	1	7	1	8	2	19	0
Baker	-	-	-	-	5	0	25	0

LANCASHIRE WON BY AN INNINGS AND 452 RUNS.

MacLaren's innings, still the highest played in first-class cricket in England was composed of one six, 62 fours, 11 threes, 37 twos and 63 singles. He and Ward put on 141 for the first wicket and then, with Paul, 363 were added in 190 minutes for the second. MacLaren was seventh out at 792.

He hit three more centuries that summer after his Taunton triumph – and they were made successively in eight days – but it was at the Oval that he showed that he was as capable of playing a dominating innings on a bad wicket as well as on a good one. On a tricky pitch Lancashire were put in to bat, and MacLaren made 52 against the formidable Surrey bowling array of Lohmann, Richardson, Lockwood, Hayward and Brockwell. This innings gave Lancashire sufficient runs for Briggs and Mold to demolish the Surrey batting and win the game. As a reward for his services to the county's cricket, the Committee elected him to life membership of the club and presented him with a gold watch.

MacLaren led the Lancashire side through the successful seasons of 1900 to 1907, and in 1904 they were unbeaten champions. His first class career spanned the years between 1890 and 1914, and in that period he scored 15,735 runs in 307 matches for Lancashire at an average of 33. These figures seem modest in comparison with the records of modern batsmen, until it is remembered that MacLaren played his cricket on pitches of variable quality, and frequently they were quite terrible. The best bowling brought out the best in his batting, and it is worthy of note that in Gentlemen v Players matches his average was 45.

There is a fine portrait in oils which hangs in the long room of the pavilion at Old Trafford, that shows admirably the sort of man MacLaren was. Cast in the classic mould, one of nature's aristocrats, his cricket reflected his personality. H.S.Altham wrote that he was one of the few cricketers to have raised batting from an accomplishment to an art. His bearing had authority, with more than a touch of hauteur, and his strokes were fashioned in the imperial manner. Sir Neville Cardus has written that he, 'dismissed the ball from his presence.' Whether he were making a 'duck' or a hundred no one can have made it so majestically as Archie MacLaren.

Contemporary photographs catch the upright stance, left shoulder to the bowler, his high back-lift and full follow-through. In his tender years, 'Monkey' Hornby had advised him to keep his left shoulder up and say his prayers, and MacLaren was always scathingly critical of the two-eyed stance, so prevalent in the cricket of the nineteen-twenties.

He had all the strokes and he was never loth to use them. MacLaren was not one who believed in hiding his light under a bushel. He was a magnificent straight-driver, though his off-drive could not match the grace of Spooner's. He could square-cut savagely or late-cut delicately, hook the ball aggressively or contemptuously from his eyebrows, but his real strength lay in his back-play, attacking back-play in which the dead-bat technique, again a fashion of later years, had no place.

C.B. Fry, his great contemporary, said of him – 'Stepping back decidedly with his right foot, his bat held rather high, he comes down plumb on the ball with a distinct, though nicely modulated swing. The bat meets the ball with no compromise.'

He scored many of his runs by forcing good-length balls away to the on-side, with a slight turn of the body and a flick of his powerful wrists. He was a player for the big occasion, and his batting thrived when the odds were against his side and the wicket was helping the bowlers. In the Lord's Test Match of 1899, the only one of the series in which there was a result and in which England were thoroughly outplayed by the Australians, MacLaren who was captaining England, saved the innings defeat with Tom Hayward. His unbeaten 88 was a splendid gesture of defiance, a proud flag nailed to the mast of a foundering ship. In the Gentlemen v Players match at Lord's in 1903, the Gentlemen followed on 293 runs behind. MacLaren joined C.B.Fry with the score at 190 for 2 and they put on 309 for the third wicket in less than three hours. Modern batsmen would be aghast at the achievement.

MacLaren played 35 times for England between 1894 and 1909, scoring nearly 2,000 runs at an average of 33. He was a member of A.E.Stoddart's side which toured Australia during the winter of 1894/95, scoring 120 in the Test at Melbourne. Three years later, when Stoddart took another side to Australia, MacLaren hit Test hundreds at Sydney and Adelaide. In 1901/2 MacLaren accepted an invitation which the M.C.C. had earlier declined, and took out a team which was not really representative in batting, since, with the exception of MacLaren himself, none of the leading amateur batsmen was able to tour. The bowling was seriously weakened when Hirst and Rhodes were prevented by pressure from the Yorkshire Committee from undertaking the tour, and, though MacLaren, with a touch of genius, championed the claims of S.F.Barnes and was splendidly vindicated by Barnes's performance in the early Tests, Barnes broke down in the third Test at Sydney and could play no further part in the series. In consequence, on a wicket which Barnes could have exploited decisively Australia succeeded in making the 315 runs they needed to win in the last innings, went into a 2 – 1 lead and won the last two Tests in Barnes's absence. MacLaren scored a century in the Sydney Test, two hundreds against New South Wales at Sydney and another against Victoria at Melbourne. His last century innings against Australia was played at Trent Bridge in 1905. He and Hayward put on 145 for the first wicket, and MacLaren went on to make a masterly 140.

Curiously enough MacLaren was a better batsman in Australia than on his native English wickets. His average for his three tours topped 50, and Australians rated him one of the finest-ever English batsmen on their wickets. He was subject to rheumatism, and doubtless the warmer, drier climate of the Antipodes exerted an improving influence on his play as well as on his health.

MacLaren captained England in 22 Test Matches, but his captaincy was sometimes open to criticism. He was a lone wolf, and he never had a particularly high opinion of Selection Committees, either during his playing days or after his retirement from the game. A Selection Committee of one member, and that member Archie MacLaren, would have suited him admirably. It was said that he was intolerant and lacking in humour. Certainly he was a stern cricketer, and this particular characteristic coloured his captaincy. Though he would not have been prepared to argue that humour has no place in cricket, he would be perfectly happy to leave that aspect of the game to others; such distractions were not for his essentially purposeful mind. As for his intolerance, it was the intolerance of the dedicated player, who expected all who professed themselves to be cricketers to treat the game seriously and to play it for all they were worth.

MacLaren was a great student of the game, a wise strategist and a shrewd tactician. His approach to an innings was predetermined, but whatever methods he adopted to achieve his ends, his aim was always the same – to prevent the bowler getting on top. As captain, in the field, he had few equals. He knew precisely the capabilities and potentialities of his bowlers, and the strengths and weaknesses of every batsman he had played with or against were tidily docketed in his mind. His favourite strategy was to feed the stroke for which the batsman had a known partiality, and so lure him to complacent destruction, rather than to block it and enourage his vigilance. As a fieldsman he always set a splendid example, which he expected to be faithfully followed. He was one of the finest slip-fielders of his time, and in his earlier days he was a brilliant out-field.

It was said, possibly by those who did not know him, that MacLaren was an optimist in his private life but a pessimist in his cricket. Certainly optimism in his private and business affairs was a pronounced characteristic. He would propound the most grandiose schemes, and if they came to naught, he could always find a horse to recoup his losses.

The events at Eastbourne at the close of the 1921 season do not bear out the contention that he was a pessimist in his cricket. The all-conquering Australians, who had been touring England that summer under Warwick Armstrong, had won the Test series with some ease. Gregory and McDonald (afterwards to play for Lancashire) had wreaked havoc among the English batsmen, and it seemed as certain as anything could be that the tourists would end their tour without being beaten.

MacLaren, who had retired from active cricket, declared that he could pick a team to beat the triumphant Australians. He picked his team, calling it 'An England XI'. It was composed entirely of amateurs, and at Eastbourne it gloriously fulfilled MacLaren's prediction against all expectations of the experts, winning the game by 28 runs, after being put out for 43 in the first innings.

Like 'Monkey' Hornby, Archie MacLaren was a tremendous force in Lancashire cricket. When his playing days were over, he could often be found in the dining room or the pavilion at Old Trafford, demonstrating with a succession of salt and pepper pots or anything else that came to hand, just how he would set a field for some batsman the Lancashire bowlers might be having some difficulty in containing. Cricketers of the stamp of A.C. MacLaren walk the cricket fields of England only once or twice in a lifetime. That portrait in the Old Trafford pavilion is at once a tribute to his cricket and a reminder of his genius.

VII

J. T. Tyldesley

The Old Trafford records reveal that in 1894, the year of poor Johnny Briggs's ill-starred benefit, a young batsman with the unmistakably Lancashire name of John Thomas Tyldesley played a highly promising innings of 75 in a second team game during the month of August. This young man was subsequently to score a great many more runs to make his name honoured and renowned in Lancashire and England cricket.

In the following season, after several more noteworthy performances with the second eleven, Tyldesley was promoted to the senior side for the match with Gloucestershire at Old Trafford. He scored 33 not out in Lancashire's second innings, and in the following game against Warwickshire at Edgbaston, 152 not out. This meritorious beginning was not maintained through all the ten matches he played for the county side that season, but *Wisden* in its review of the year recorded, 'the general impression seemed to be that he had a good deal of cricket in him.'

Young John Thomas had a quieter season in 1896, but in 1897 he again showed his liking for the Edgbaston wicket with a century in each innings of Lancashire's game with Warwickshire, followed by 174 against Sussex at Old Trafford. It was in 1898, however, that it could truly be said that a great batsman had arrived. Lancashire did not enjoy a particularly successful season, but on the brighter side, Tyldesley scored nearly 2,000 runs in all first-class matches. He hit a hundred at Canterbury and shared with MacLaren in a partnership of 155 in two hours. In the Derbyshire match at Old Trafford he made his first double century, helping Lancashire to a score of 464 for 7 wickets, made in 270 minutes on the opening day.

Test recognition followed in 1899 when Tyldesley played twice for England, the first of his 31 appearances for his country. From then until 1909, he was an automatic choice for Test sides, and in 1902 he was the only professional to be picked for his batting alone in a year when the England team included some of the finest amateur talent ever to grace it.

When the Australians played Lancashire at Old Trafford the members and spectators were privileged to see in action Victor Trumper and Johnny Tyldesley, two of the most brilliant stroke-makers of all time on difficult wickets. Trumper made 82, Tyldesley 56 out of 102 in Lancashire's first innings and 42 out of 81 in the second.

Sir Neville Cardus has likened Tyldesley's bat to an honest broadsword, drawn in the service of Lancashire. Tyldesley would certainly not have thought of it in such metaphorical terms, but he would surely have been in full agreement with the implications of Sir Neville's felicitous phrasing. He was one of nature's craftsmen, a true professional who would have been ashamed to take his money if his job were not well done. If his cutting were sheer poetry, he and possibly he alone would not be conscious of the artistry of it, but he would be acutely aware of the craftsmanship. The analogy of the honest broadsword is as appropriate as that of the rapier to Spooner's bat or the sabre to MacLaren's.

Tyldesley commanded the complete armoury of strokes, and in a long innings he would use them all with telling effect. If the cut, and particularly the square cut were the most stylish strokes in his repertoire and the ones that everyone most liked to see him play, he was the acknowledged master, too, of the drive, the hook and the forcing shot off the back foot. Those who saw his square cut were unlikely to forget it. He would move across the stumps like lightning, and, head over the ball, exert all his weight into the stroke, cracking it, more often than not, to the boundary, almost before the fieldsmen could move a muscle.

Quickness of foot, keenness of eye and perfect body balance were the foundations of Tyldesley's superb technique. He would recommend young players to follow the example of his own younger days, and to spend as many of their evenings as they could in the ballroom during the winter months. Dancing, he would say, had helped him enormously in retaining his balance, his suppleness and his nimbleness of foot.

Few batsmen in the history of cricket could compare with Johnny Tyldesley on bad wickets. On a pitch giving every assistance to the bowlers, most batsmen would be content to survive by defensive, dead-bat play. Not Tyldesley. He believed that the policy most likely to succeed on a difficult wicket was to attack, and to attack in such a positive way that the ball was cracked as far away from the stumps as possible.

Tyldesley learned his craft in what has become known as the classical period of English cricket. The bowlers he was called upon to face were masters of their art – such men as G.A. Lohmann, Tom Richardson, Bobby Peel, Monty Noble, and J.T. Hearne. The new googly bowling, introduced by the South Africans, Schwarz, Vogler, White, Pegler and Faulkner presented no terrors to him. He was one of the first batsmen to master it, as he mastered all the changes in bowling fashion which were evolved during his cricketing career. To his native shrewdness there was allied a vigilance at the wicket that made him at once the despair of the honest trundlers who trundled for a living, and of the amateur who trundled for the enjoyment of it. Yet, one might think, what enjoyment could be derived by a bowler, be he amateur or professional, who started from his mark to see Johnny Tyldesley's bat at the other end, waiting to inflict the direst punishment upon him and to thwart his every stratagem and artifice? The batsman's stumps must have seemed twice their distance away from him.

Cricket writers since the beginning of the century have recognized an innings by Tyldesley in the Second Test at Melbourne in the 1903-4 series as one of the really great innings of cricket history. England had batted first on a fast wicket and Tyldesley was highest scorer with 97 in a total that topped 300. The remainder of the match was played between rainstorms on a wicket which had become spiteful in the extreme. Despite a fine innings of 74 by Trumper, who was missed at 3, the Australians could make little of Rhodes and could only manage 122 in reply. The wicket had deteriorated so much when England began their second knock that the word 'impossible' ascribed to it by the cricket historians, seems not inappropriate. The bowlers made the ball come through at varying awkward heights, Trumble especially making it rise straight from a length. Tyldesley played the most superb innings on that cauldron of a wicket, scoring 62 of England's 103. Only half of the other batsmen made double figures.

The Australians had not the slightest chance of making the 287 runs they needed to win, and had the English fieldsmen not been so generous in putting down as many as eight chances, they would have been put out for considerably less than the 111 they ultimately achieved.

Between 1899 and 1909 Tyldesley scored 1,66l runs in Test matches at an average of 30.75. There are England batsmen enough who have made more runs at better averages, but it should be remembered that Tyldesley's runs were made against top-class bowling on indifferent wickets. He hit three centuries against Australia – at Edgbaston in 1902 and two in 1905 at Leeds and the Oval. His fourth Test hundred, the first in sequence, was made at Cape Town in Lord Hawke's South African tour of 1898/99.

Tyldesley's commanding batsmanship was seen at its best in the England – Australian series of 1905. In the first Test at Trent Bridge, on a damp wicket, he was top scorer with 56 of England's first innings total of 196. Cotter and Laver were in hostile mood, making the ball fly spitefully, but Tyldesley never flinched from the thunderbolts hurled at him, playing his strokes with unhurried calm and immaculate care. Australia went to a modest first innings lead, but MacLaren and Hayward put England in a strong position at the start of the second innings, sharing in an opening stand of 145.

All hopes of a win were abandoned by the Australians whilst MacLaren and Hayward were consolidating England's position, and in an attempt to secure a draw Armstrong bowled wide of the batsman's legs to a constricting leg side field. This stratagem was ingeniously thwarted by Tyldesley who stepped smartly away from his wicket in the direction of square-leg and cracked the ball through the sparse off-field. Only a batsman with Johnny Tyldesley's adroitness of foot could have conceived and executed this brilliant counterstroke. Tyldesley made 61, but more important to England's cause than the number of runs he scored was the maintenance of a brisk scoring rate, which Jackson and Rhodes were able to build upon the following morning.

Australia were set to score 402 to win, but after a solid start by Darling and Duff, their batting collapsed before the bowling of Bosanquet. Victor Trumper, who had been obliged to retire with a strained back in the first innings, made a valiant attempt to reach the crease after the fall of the ninth wicket, but he could get no further than the pavilion gate and England had won comfortably.

At Leeds, in the third Test, Armstrong again bowled wide of

the leg-stump in England's second innings. Fifty-one overs of it effectively neutralized the first-innings lead and postponed a declaration until almost one o'clock on the last day. Tyldesley scored a fine hundred by adopting the same tactics he had used so successfully at Nottingham, but none of the other England batsmen was nimble enough of foot to emulate him.

After England had made the series and the 'Ashes' safe with an innings victory at Old Trafford on a rain-affected wicket, Tyldesley showed his mastery again in the second innings of the fifth Test at the Oval. C.B. Fry had thrilled the crowd in England's first innings with a brilliant century which H.S. Altham described as 'as attractive an innings as he had ever played'. His off-driving and cutting that day brought pleasure to the eyes and took away the breath.

The Australians were only 70 behind England's total of 430, thanks to another brilliant innings, this time by Duff. On the last morning, when England went in again, Fry, Hayward and MacLaren were dismissed for only 13 runs, but Tyldesley, first in partnership with Jackson and then with Spooner, halted the Australian bowlers firmly in their tracks. He hit an unbeaten 112, and his exhilarating association with Spooner added 158 runs in 80 minutes. These three innings, of Fry, Duff and Tyldesley, sharply contrasted in style and character, but each an unforgettable experience of batting artistry were outstanding in a drawn game.

But it is as a Lancashire cricketer that Johnny Tyldesley is primarily remembered in these pages. His record for the county is astonishing. He scored nearly 32,000 runs at an average of 41. His younger brother Ernest scored 2,000 more runs, but he played 66 more innings than Johnny. For nineteen years in succession Johnny scored more than a thousand runs, four times he exceeded 2,000 and once (in 1901) he topped 3,000. His list of centuries includes hundreds against every county then playing in the Championship. At Edgbaston, always a happy hunting ground, his performances were legendary. There he scored no less than eleven centuries in county and representatives games. Curiously enough, his partiality for making runs on the Birmingham ground was shared by his brother Ernest. The Warwickshire bowlers of his day must have felt that they had achieved a major break-through whenever they sent Johnny Tyldesley back to the pavilion cheaply.

Tyldesley's highest innings (295) was played in 1906 at Old Trafford against Kent, who were county champions that year. According to the records the Lancashire total reached 531 at the rate of a hundred an hour. In the previous season at Trent Bridge, he had played an innings of 250 in under six hours, during which every Nottinghamshire player had bowled at him.

Twice he hit two centuries in a match – against Warwickshire at Edgbaston in 1897 and against Hampshire at Old Trafford in 1910. In 1897 and again in 1904 he hit three hundreds in successive innings and he still shares with Archie MacLaren the record Lancashire fourth wicket partnership – 324 against Notts at Trent Bridge in 1904. Though a glittering string of eighty-six centuries spanned his first-class career, many of his best innings were played on sticky wickets for more modest scores.

When the first world war broke out Tyldesley was nearly forty. He lost four summers, and when cricket was resumed at county level in 1919, he played only one full season more. It is reasonable to assume that had those war years not been lost to him, he would have achieved his hundred hundreds, and many another honour besides.

Several of the Lancashire players joined the forces when hostilities began, but Tyldesley, who had then passed forty, was too old for service. He was much too immersed in his cricket to put it aside for the duration, so he kept himself in trim and his batting in prime condition by organizing matches in all parts of the country for war charities.

When he finally retired from active cricket in 1923, Tyldesley's aggregate of over 37,000 runs in all matches had, to that time, been exceeded only by W.G. Grace and Tom Hayward.

As a deep fieldsman Tyldesley had few peers. Here his winter ballroom training helped again. He was quick in movement, sure in anticipation, a safe catch and a magnificent thrower.

To my lasting regret I never saw J.T. Tyldesley in the middle. If it were possible for a good fairy to grant me three wishes, this would be one that I should ask to be fulfilled and preferably that I could see him play over again that splendidly defiant innings in the Second Test at Melbourne in 1903.

He had begun a new career as coach to the Lancashire county club when I first began to watch cricket at Old Trafford. One of my earliest boyhood recollections is of seeing him at the nets with the young members of the ground staff, a compact little figure, still splendidly supple though his hair and moustache had turned white. He was demonstrating to the youngsters with a bat of well-seasoned willow, how he had fashioned those glorious strokes which so excited the crowds in his heyday and gave such lustre to the game.

VIII

R.H. Spooner

Reginald Herbert Spooner will always occupy a distinguished, even a hallowed place in Lancashire cricket history. He was the epitome of elegance and grace, one of the loveliest stroke players cricket has ever known. In 1905, *Wisden* wrote of him, 'In point of style there are few batsmen of the present day to compare with him. Not even L.C.H. Palairet himself is better worth looking at. Style in batting is not thought so much of now as it was years ago, but it certainly makes for enjoyment.'

Every stroke Spooner made at the wicket, indeed his every movement was carried through easily and gracefully, but his particular glories and the strokes for which he was justly renowned were the off-drive and the cover drive. Both were shots of sheer beauty to be savoured, treasured and recalled nostalgically when the past is remembered.

Though Spooner's off-drive is classed by the connoisseur with that of Palairet as the ultimate in perfection, there was a marked difference in their execution. Palairet's was a model of orthodoxy, performed with a free swing of the bat and follow through. Spooner's began in the orthodox way, but at the last moment a quick flick of his wrists imparted to the stroke a magical quality of seemingly effortless power.

Whilst Spooner was at Marlborough, he was rated the school's finest batsman since A.G. Steel. In his last year he scored 926 runs at an average of 71 and topped the batting averages. He was, at that time, also a useful bowler, second in the bowling averages and always capable of taking wickets with slow, seemingly innocuous deliveries. He made his first appearance for Lancashire in 1899, his final year at Marlborough, in the match against Middlesex at Lord's, where he had already that season scored 69 and 198 for the school against the traditional enemy, Rugby. It is said that he treated J.T. Hearne and Albert Trott, the formidable Middlesex bowlers in the same cavalier fashion as he had treated the bowlers he had met at Marlborough in his schooldays. He opened the Lancashire batting with Ward, scoring 44 in the first innings and 83 in the second. Johnny Tyldesley who had particularly warned the youngster about the guile of Albert Trott and exhorted him especially to watch above all else for his slower ball, twice succumbed rather easily to that very ball, whilst the novice (but not such a novice as that!) was making his runs.

Though he had left school, Spooner was unable to play for Lancashire in the following season, as he was stationed with the militia in Ireland, and it was not until 1903, after he had served in the Boer War in South Africa, that the cricket fields of England saw him again. Business commitments restricted drastically the time he could devote to cricket, and only in six seasons was he able to play regularly.

His business commitments also prevented his going to Australia, though he received several invitations to tour. He was asked to captain the 1920-21 side, but he was obliged to decline, and the team went out under the captaincy of J.W.H.T. Douglas. Australians would have relished his cultured style, and the Australian wickets would have suited Spooner down to the ground.

Though it has been argued that he was essentially a fast-wicket batsman and that he was not so effective against the ball that deviated as it came to the bat, the theorists of this school appear to overlook the fact that he was one of the first batsmen to read the googly and to play it with confidence. In the Triangular Tournament in 1912, Spooner scored 119 in 3 hours in the Lord's Test off an attack which included Faulkner, Pegler and Schwarz. *Wisden* in paying tribute to this innings, also gave high tribute to Spooner's forcing back play.

He had learned to bat against bowling directed mainly on or to the off-side of the stumps. The more modern tendency to aim defensively at the leg stump or outside it distressed Spooner greatly when he saw it in his later years, and he would often say that if similar tactics had been used in his day, he could have done no good with them. It would have been impossible to drive such bowling past cover.

One feels that this self-stricture could never have applied to such a fine batsman as Reggie Spooner. Though his glorious cover-drive would have been cruelly restricted, there were still sufficient strokes in his repertoire to have brought him abundant runs in his own supremely graceful fashion.

He could drive the fastest bowling with tremendous power, generated by his strong shoulders and supple wrists. I once saw Peter May drive Brian Statham thus to the sight-screen at Old Trafford, and as the ball thumped against the woodwork, an elderly member sitting next to me, murmured that the stroke reminded him of Reggie Spooner in his prime. I was born too late to see Spooner bat, but for me there could be no higher tribute to his greatness.

The records of the fine innings he played can, of course, give no indication of the superbly elegant batting he brought to them. In 1910 he scored 200 not out against Yorkshire at Old Trafford, still the highest score made by a Lancashire player in the matches between the two counties.

The match had been set aside for Jack Sharp's benefit. Yorkshire were all out for 103 in their first innings; Walter Brearley who took 5 wickets for 50 runs would have had an even better analysis, but for an obdurate innings from George Herbert Hirst, who stepped valiantly into the breach after half his side's wickets had gone for 34.

All that had happened previously paled, however, before the scintillating brilliance of Spooner. Runs flowed in rich profusion from his bat, so that Sir Neville Cardus who saw his innings that day was moved to write that he, 'changed Old Trafford's turf into textures of silk or gold.'

The Yorkshire bowlers could do nothing with him and their captain could set no field to contain him. When Spooner reached his double century, A.H. Hornby who was captaining Lancashire, declared, nearly 300 runs ahead, and Brearley and Dean with plenty of runs to bowl at, saw Yorkshire to defeat by an innings. Unfortunately Spooner could not appear regularly throughout that summer, and he scored only about 600 runs in the 22 innings he played.

Spooner first played for England in the fourth Test at Old Trafford in 1905 against Australia. He scored 52 in a game which the Australians lost by an innings. In the last Test at the Oval he was dismissed without scoring in England's first innings, bowled by Cotter by a ball that he failed to pick out against the gloom of the pavilion. In the second innings he adequately atoned for his failure, delighting the crowd with a dazzling 79 in as many minutes, and sharing with Johnny Tyldesley in a stand of 158. In his ten Test matches he scored 481 runs at an average of

32. That he took part in so little Test cricket when he had so much to give to it seems a sad waste of talent.

Spooner played several times in Gentlemen v Players matches, and his innings of 114 in 1906 at Lord's is still rated one of the finest ever played for the Gentlemen in these annual encounters which are today only a part of cricket's history. It was an innings for the connoisseur of cricket as well as for the connoisseur of beauty. *Wisden*, describing it, said, 'Spooner played one of the finest innings of his life. Better batting was not seen at Lord's all the season. Powerful on-driving and very skilful play on the leg-side were the features of his innings.'

One comes, as one always must, in assessing a cricketer's career, to statistics, though in Spooner's case they can tell only a part of the tale. For Lancashire between 1899 and 1921 he played in 170 matches and scored 9889 runs at an average of 37. In all matches he made 13,396 runs at an average of 36. These included 31 centuries, 25 of them for Lancashire. The stark figures cannot conjure up the brilliance of his stroke-play or the pleasure it brought to those who were privileged to see it. They assume more significance, perhaps, when one reflects that for Lancashire his average is four above Archie MacLaren's and only four less than Johnny Tyldesley's.

In 1903 MacLaren and Spooner scored 368 for Lancashire's first wicket against Gloucestershire at Aigburth, a club record which still stands.

As a fieldsman he was rated, at cover, one of the greatest in the game. When one admires cover-fielding at Old Trafford in these latter days, there is usually close at hand an older member who will turn to you sympathetically and say, with the light in his eye of one who has seen visions, if not dreamed dreams, 'Ah, but you could not have seen Reggie Spooner.'

Spooner's fielding had an ease and grace, like to his batting, and his throw was swift, powerful and accurate. He was often compared with the great Vernon Royle at Old Trafford, and if those who saw both field at cover said that no one could attain Royle's overall brilliance, Spooner could not have been very far below it.

Sir Neville Cardus has said that Spooner was one of the cricketers who, when he was a boy, made him fall in love with the game. For that he has earned the gratitude, not only of Cardus himself, but of everyone who loves cricket.

In December 1944, during the second World War, when he was installed as President of the County Club, Spooner in a moment of great emotion, spoke of his readiness to help in whatever way he could with the restoration of the bomb-damaged Old Trafford ground and added almost as an aside, 'Would to God we could put the clock back!'

Would to God we could! Spooner may have been vainly sighing for the salad days of his cricketing prime, but if time could really move backwards what a feast of cricket there would be for those of us who never saw Reggie Spooner and Archie MacLaren going forth from the pavilion to open a Lancashire innings. And with Johnny Tyldesley at Number three, waiting in the pavilion in his pads, what more could life have to offer?

IX

Walter Brearley

Walter Brearley was one of the most tempestuous cricketers ever to wear the red rose crest, a Falstaffian figure who played his cricket with vigorous enthusiasm, was never loth to tilt at authority and well merited the reputation he gained at Old Trafford as a 'reet character'. Brearley played no first-class cricket until he was twenty-six years of age, though he had played a fair amount of club cricket, gaining a reputation as a fast bowler, first with Bolton and then with Manchester.

He played his first game for the county side at Brighton in 1902, but his start was modest, and it was not until the following season, when he played in fifteen games that he created any impression. He took 69 wickets at 23 runs apiece, and though he did not maintain throughout the season his excellent form of the earlier months, his zest and capacity for sustained effort earned him a place in the Gentlemen's team at Lord's. He performed reasonably well, though all else in the game was transcended by the brilliant partnership of MacLaren and Fry who together scored 309 in under three hours on a far from perfect wicket. When Surrey came to Old Trafford Brearley and Sydney Barnes shared all twenty wickets, and in the 'roses' game there Brearley, who was to be an embarrassment to Yorkshire for most of his career, not only played the main part in avoiding a Lancashire follow on, but continued his assault with the ball and proceeded to shed petals from the white rose with a devastating spell of bowling in which he took 6 wickets for 81 runs.

It was in 1904, however, when Lancashire ran away with the Championship, that Brearley really came into his own. His bowling advanced so well that by the end of the season he was considered the best amateur fast bowler in the country. He would have taken more wickets than he did (95 in all matches at 20 apiece), had he not missed several of Lancashire's August matches through injury.

Unfortunately the season ended with Brearley's first brush

with authority. He was left out of the Lancashire side for the Champion County v The Rest of England game and announced his retirement from county cricket. Happily for all, the matter was settled amicably before the start of the 1905 season, and when cricket was resumed at Old Trafford, Brearley was there, the scent of battle in his nostrils, his zest for the game as sharp as ever.

Surely 1905 must have been Walter Brearley's finest season. For Lancashire he took 133 wickets at 19 runs apiece, in all matches 181 at substantially the same average. The nature of his achievement must be measured against the fact that he and Kermode were virtually Lancashire's bowling that season; the indifferent form of the other bowlers threw a good deal of extra work on their shoulders. Not that Walter Brearley ever grumbled about hard work. He was willing to bowl all day and every day, and if the rules had permitted it, he would have bowled at both ends for as long as he could have remained on his feet.

Undoubtedly his finest performance was in the Somerset match at Old Trafford when he took 9 wickets for 47 runs before lunch on the first day. In this astonishing day's cricket Somerset were dismissed for 65, and Lancashire replied with 424 for 8 before the drawing of stumps. When Somerset batted again, Brearley accomplished the remarkable performance of taking 4 wickets in four balls. He had finished off the first innings with two wickets from successive balls, and he began the second innings with a similar feat. He went on to take 8 wickets for 90 in the innings, a formidable match analysis of 17 for 137.

When the Australians visited Old Trafford, Brearley came down like a wolf on the fold and took 7 of their wickets for 115 runs.

There was a spot of bother when Gloucestershire came north. When Brearley batted in Lancashire's innings there had been a certain amount of banter and a joke had gone wrong. Tempers became ruffled after Gloucestershire had lost 3 wickets for 47 runs and Jessop and Board, in an attempt to hit their side out of trouble, launched a violent assault on the Lancashire bowling. In four overs 57 runs were scored, and the two batsmen added 98 in 40 minutes. Brearley retaliated by bowling fast full-tosses, some of them head high. He ultimately dismissed both batsmen and Lancashire won comfortably, but the unpleasantness which had been engendered lasted for several weeks. Jessop is said to have threatened never to play again at Old Trafford, but the storm blew over and the sores were healed before the teams met again.

In the 'roses' game at Old Trafford, after Spooner and Tyldesley had enchanted the crowd on Whit Monday with a stand of 253 for Lancashire's second wicket, there was rain early on the Tuesday morning and Yorkshire were soon in the toils. Brearley and Kermode caused the ball to rear and kick unpleasantly and they sent the Old Enemy to an innings defeat. Yorkshire took their revenge in the return game at Bramall Lane in August, though not before Brearley had shocked them again in their first innings, gobbling up seven of their batsmen, with the nonchalant air of a man taking a light appetiser before looking around for the main course.

It was inevitable, on Brearley's record that summer that he should gain Test recognition against the Australians, though he played in only the last two Tests, at Old Trafford and the Oval. In both these matches Lancashire had four representatives – MacLaren, Johnny Tyldesley, Spooner and Brearley. Brearley acquitted himself well on his own midden. He took 4 wickets (Trumper, Noble, Duff and McLeod) for 72 runs in Australia's first innings and 4 for 54 (Noble, Armstrong, Duff and Darling) in the second, helping England to an innings victory.

At the Oval, in a magnificent piece of bowling he took 5 wickets for 110 runs in 31 overs in Australia's first innings, his victims Trumper, Hill, Hopkins, McLeod and Cotter. There were only 2½ hours of play left when the Australians began their second innings, requiring 329 to win and a draw was well nigh a certainty, so that the rest of the proceedings were more academic than vital. Brearley, however, again took the wicket of Trumper, caught at the wicket by Spooner, who was, in fact substituting for the injured Lilley.

In after years, whenever the praises of Victor Trumper were being extolled, Brearley would claim the great Australian as his 'rabbit'. Certainly his record against Trumper when the two were in opposition in that summer of 1905 does not tend to disprove this assessment. Brearley bowled against Trumper in nine innings, spread over five matches and on six occasions he took his wicket for less than 30. The full record may be of interest:-

Australians v Gentlemen of England at Crystal Palace
    V.T.Trumper b Brearley   2

Australians v Gentlemen of England at Lord's
    V.T.Trumper b Brearley   4

Australians v Lancashire at Old Trafford
    V.T.Trumper b Brearley   14

Fourth Test Match at Old Trafford
    V.T.Trumper c Rhodes b Brearley   11

Fifth Test Match at the Oval
    V.T.Trumper b Brearley 4 c Spooner b Brearley   28.

Apparently there was a further difference of opinion or a sense of grievance at the end of the season, for Brearley again submitted his resignation. Once more he was back in the spring, but he played in only five matches during the following season. Lancashire sorely missed his bowling and dropped from second to fourth place in the Championship. Had he played they must surely have finished higher, and might easily have taken Kent's place as county champions.

It was not until 1908 that Brearley returned as a regular member to the Lancashire side, and he celebrated his return by taking 148 wickets in 17 Championship matches at 15 runs apiece. Despite this achievement Lancashire had an indifferent season and clearly Brearley and Dean had too much bowling to do. Both were bowlers who thrived on hard work, but they did not have the support they were entitled to expect. The wickets at Old Trafford that year were described as 'fast and dangerous', and as Brearley flung himself into his bowling with all his customary energy and vigour, it is perhaps not surprising that he was chosen as one of *Wisden*'s 'Five Cricketers of the Year'.

Again the Yorkshire batsmen felt the power of his strong right arm. In the Old Trafford game he bowled 60 overs, to take 13 wickets for 196 runs in their two innings, but his lion-hearted bowling could not halt the flow of the Yorkshire tide to victory. Against Essex at Old Trafford he had the remarkable match analysis of 14 wickets for 111 runs.

In 1909 Lancashire had a much more successful season, finishing second to Kent in the Championship, and Brearley took 118 wickets in Championship games at 16 apiece. He went through the Yorkshire first innings like a forest fire in the 'roses' game at Old Trafford, finishing with 9 wickets for 80 runs, but again his performance could not prevent a Lancashire defeat. The four completed innings in this match totalled only 357 runs.

Brearley had another brush with authority when, on the first morning of the second Test at Lord's he was approached by Archie MacLaren to play for England, as the bowling was considered to be too weak. Brearley, however, was of the firm opinion that he had been slighted by not being picked for the original side selected and he refused the invitation.

In 1910 injury limited Brearley's appearances to three games, one of which was the 'roses' match at Old Trafford. He took half the wickets in Yorkshire's first innings, and after Spooner and Johnny Tyldesley had seen Lancashire into a strong position, he and Dean again mopped up the Yorkshire batting to give Lancashire an innings win.

In 1911 also, he was unable to play regularly, and in what was to be his last season with the county, he bowled only 417 overs, but took 79 wickets at 19 runs apiece. There were searing flashes of his old zest and zip. In the Somerset match at Aigburth he had a match analysis of 14 wickets for 142 and at Old Trafford he wrecked a Gloucestershire innings with 8 for 109. The very sight of the white rose on the caps of the Yorkshire batsmen at Old Trafford was sufficient to inspire him to another splendid performance against the Old Enemy, his farewell to 'roses' cricket. At 46, though the flesh was weakening, the will and the spirit never knew the meaning of the word 'enough'.

Walter Brearley's physical fitness was proverbial. Going out to bat, he would often leap the gate leading from the pavilion to the field; by this antic he was certainly not implying that the gate should remain closed since he intended to stay in the middle for an hour or so. Quite the contrary. As a batsman Brearley rarely troubled the scorers very much and Gilbert Jessop wasn't very far wrong when he said that before Walter went out to bat, he would light a cigarette, leave it burning in an ashtray and have a more than even chance of being back in time fo finish smoking it before the tobacco had burned through. It is said that he could vault a full-sized billiard table, and I once spoke to a man who claimed to have seen him do it.

Brearley's bowling run was short – a mere eight paces – but his speed came from his powerful shoulders and full follow-through. He made subtle use of the width of the crease, delivering balls from several different points during the course of an over, so that although there appeared no variation from the ring, the batsman, at least, was well aware of the differences of direction. He could bring the ball back or bowl the outswinger, and he could get life and lift out of most wickets. On the natural Old Trafford wickets of the pre-1914 era he could make batsmen very uncomfortable indeed.

He did not bowl merely to cause batsmen discomfort, however. He bowled to get them out; so far as he was concerned they had no good right to be occupying the crease at all, and the sooner they were back in the pavilion, the better for everybody. It was his firm conviction, too, that no one was better equipped than he to administer the *coup-de-grâce*.

There can be no more admirable quality in a bowler, particularly a fast one. He thrived on the big occasion and no one enjoyed the 'roses' matches more than he. The white rose of Yorkshire aroused the devil in him. His record in these games speaks for itself – 125 wickets in 14 matches at a cost of only 16 runs each.

His quarrels and feuds were legion. He was quick to take offence, where none was intended. The Committee members were not immune from the sharp edge of his tongue; there were frequent differences, threats of retirement, even retirements, but he usually cooled as quickly as he had come to the boil, and fortunately for Lancashire cricket the breaches were mended before they became permanent. For the county in his all-too-brief first class career he took 690 wickets at 18.7 runs each in 106 matches. He played for England in four Tests, taking 17 wickets at 21 runs apiece. Walter Brearley brought a fresh breeze to Lancashire's matches in Edwardian days, and Old Trafford was always a livelier place for his presence and for the cricket he played there.

Sir Neville Cardus in his pen-picture of Brearley imagines him in the cricketers' happy hunting-ground beyond the Styx, bowling for ever at a wicket defended by W.G. Grace, the greatest batsman of all against fast bowlers. I like to think that,

GEORGE DUCKWORTH claims another victim
(*L.C.C.C./Kemsley Newspapers*)

J.T. TYLDESLEY
(*L.C.C.C.*)

R.G. BARLOW
(L.C.C.C.)

R. POLLARD
(*L.C.C.C./News Chronicle*)

EDDIE PAYNTER
(L.C.C.C./Daily Herald)

JACK BOND
(L.C.C.C.)

CYRIL WASHBROOK
(Guardian or Fox Photos?)

ARTHUR MOLD
(L.C.C.C.)

(Standing): G. DUCKWORTH, F. WATSON, J.L. HOPWOOD, J. IDDON, F. SIBBLES, G. HODGSON, E. PAYNTER

(Seated): C. HALLOWS, E.A. McDONALD, P.T. ECKERSLEY, (*Capt.*), E. TYLDESLEY, R. TYLDESLEY

Lancashire C.C.C. – 1930 Champions

FAROKH ENGINEER
(L.C.C.C.)

CECIL PARKIN, DICK TYLDESLEY, E.A. McDONALD

not only would Walter make one or two whistle through the Doctor's beard, but that the good Doctor's 'castle' would not be kept inviolate. Whoever should take the honours in such a titanic encounter, I know who would be the first to tire. It would not be Walter Brearley.

X

Harry Dean and 'Lol' Cook

After the retirement of Walter Brearley from first-class cricket, two of the mainstays of Lancashire's attack in the decade that followed were Harry Dean and Lawrence Cook, known at Old Trafford and hereafter in these pages as 'Lol'.

Both bowlers served the county for roughly the same time. Dean's career spanned the years between 1906 and 1921, during which he took 1267 wickets for Lancashire in 256 matches at 18 runs apiece. 'Lol' Cook played in 203 matches between 1907 and 1923, taking 821 wickets for 21 runs each.

Dean, a forthright Lancashire lad, always prepared to bowl his heart out for his side, was for some seasons one of the best bowlers in the country. He was a left-arm swerve bowler of the George Hirst type, but if the wicket suited it, he could bowl orthodox left-arm spin. A useful man to have in any side.

Harry Dean came into the Lancashire team for the first time in 1906, and in the following season he took 110 wickets at 20 runs each. His most outstanding performances that season were 8 wickets for 43 runs against the University at Oxford and 9 for 46 against Derbyshire at Chesterfield.

From then until 1913 and after the war in 1920 he regularly took his hundred wickets a season; only in 1914 when he was suffering from a troublesome knee injury which prevented his playing much cricket did he fail to achieve the hundred regarded at Old Trafford as almost his by right.

His record is formidable:-

	WICKETS	AVERAGE
1907	110	20.36
1908	129	18.14
1909	102	17.10
1910	133	15.21
1911	179	17.48
1912	136	12.51
1913	123	18.37

1920   124   16.16

In 1909 his performances in two matches stood out above all his other bowling that season. After Warwickshire had been sent in to bat at Aigburth, Dean shot out nine of their batsmen for 35 runs in their first innings, and followed up with 4 for 46 in the second. At the end of the season, he surpassed even this feat, with a match analysis of 14 for 77 against Somerset at Old Trafford.

The following season Dean shocked Somerset again when he demolished their batting on their own soil at Bath, taking 9 wickets for 77 runs in the first innings and 7 for 26 in the second.

In the lovely summer of 1911 he bowled better than ever before, getting through more overs and taking more wickets than any other bowler in the country. In the Warwickshire match at Old Trafford he took 8 wickets for 121 and against Leicestershire at Leicester 9 for 109. When Hampshire came to Old Trafford and the Lancashire batsmen flogged their bowling for 676 runs in 6½ hours, Dean and Cook carried on the good work by putting them out for 102 and 119, the biggest win ever recorded by Lancashire, and the third widest victory margin in the history of the Championship.

The softer wickets of 1912 were better suited to Dean's natural spin than to his swerve and he exploited it with telling effect. In the Kent game at Old Trafford he took 15 wickets for 108 runs, winning the match for Lancashire in the last over when he caught and bowled Colin Blythe. It was Dean, too, with 13 wickets for 49 who destroyed Worcestershire whilst at Derby he had another good match with 12 for 163. He and Huddlestone bowled unchanged at Leicester, sharing all the wickets between them.

Test recognition came that season when he was selected to play for England against Australia and South Africa in the Triangular Tournament. He played against Australia at Lord's and the Oval, but at Lord's the game was ruined by rain, and he could play little effective part. At the Oval, he and Woolley bowled England to victory in the second innings, and at Headingley he had a match analysis of 5 for 56 in the defeat of the South Africans.

The performance for which Harry Dean will always be particularly remembered at Old Trafford took place in 1913. 'In that year there were three 'roses' meetings; in addition to the two Championship games, an extra match was arranged at Aigburth as part of the celebrations in connection with the visit to

Liverpool of King George V. The game was accorded first class status and Lancashire won it by three wickets (one feels that it would have been somewhat inappropriate if Yorkshire had won a game arranged by way of a Lancashire celebration). Dean played a decisive part in the victory by taking 17 Yorkshire wickets for 91 runs – 9 for 62 in the first innings and 8 for 29 in the second. At Old Trafford we tend to judge our cricketers by their performance in 'roses' games, and this, above all his other excellencies, must rank as Harry Dean's finest hour.

Had the 1914–18 war not taken four seasons from him it is reasonable to suppose that Dean could have surpassed Johnny Briggs's record of 1688 wickets for Lancashire. He played little in 1914 – there was some difference with the Committee, apart from his injury – and when cricket was resumed in 1919 he did not have a particularly effective season, his 51 wickets costing nearly 30 runs each.

There was a return to something like his old form in 1920, his benefit year, and he took 8 Surrey wickets in an innings for 80 runs at Old Trafford, but he was overshadowed that season by his good friend and partner Lol Cook, and in the benefit match itself by Cecil Parkin. Though the benefit game (against Middlesex) was over in two days, it was successful enough financially and Harry Dean was the richer by over £2,200, a figure second only to J.T. Tyldesley's to that date.

His career was drawing to its close; his form in 1921 was indifferent and he faded from the first-class scene. He had given of his best to Lancashire cricket in rain and shine, fair weather and foul, and of all the bowlers who have served Lancashire county through the years, none has had a greater heart than Harry Dean.

The career of 'Lol' Cook, like that of Harry Dean, was interrupted by the war, and his figures tell nothing of the immense amount of hard work, often with scant material reward, that he performed in Lancashire's cause. For Cook was what is known as an 'unlucky' bowler. If, in the course of a single over, a ball of perfect length and direction missed the stumps by the merest fraction, a sharp chance was put down at slip and an unsympathetic umpire chose to turn a deaf ear to the bowler's confident appeal when the batsman's leg was plumb in front, you could be pretty certain that the unfortunate bowler who was being subjected to all these annoying frustrations was 'Lol' Cook.

Every county, at some time, has its Cook or its Dean, its honest toiler, dedicated to his job and prepared to give his all, no matter if the conditions, the elements, the umpires and even the fates themselves are against him, and whether the effort brings its reward or not. These are the conscientious cricketers, the craftsmen with an infinite capacity for taking pains. Unhappily, in this unfair world, where virtue so rarely earns its due reward, it is not these well-deserving folk, but the less direct, more subtle fellows, who are accorded the palms of genius.

Not that 'Lol' Cook would have been bothered by such philosophising. Indeed, if he had harboured such thoughts as he tramped back again and again to his bowling mark, his brow and shirt bathed in good Lancashire sweat, and the figures recorded against his name in the scorebook, one wicket for a hundred in forty overs, he would, not merely like sturdy Private Willis in 'Iolanthe', have astonished us, but most assuredly would have astonished himself.

He must, however, have realized in his formative years, that he, 'Lol' Cook, was not destined to be the favoured child of benign fortune. Everything that was to be earned must be earned by tremendously hard work and sustained application. If the rewards came in due season, well, no one could say he hadn't worked hard for them; if they didn't, why then, he had still worked hard, though scurvy fortune had seen fit to turn its back on him.

He had his grouses of course, and he was well entitled to have them. Let no one run away with the idea that 'Lol' Cook suffered the slings and arrows of outrageous fortune with a meek submissiveness. There would be a salty gibe at the batsman who had edged him perilously through the slips, a furious outburst directed at the absent varnisher of the stumps who had so obviously skimped his job, an unbelieving, pitying glance at the umpire who affected not to hear the explosive appeal delivered in the closest possible proximity to his ear-drums.

Recognition in representative cricket did not come Cook's way, and I suspect that he did not anticipate it would, having regard to all the circumstances. But he was a very good bowler all the same and he possessed the inestimable virtue of maintaining his length and direction over after over. He was one of the old school of bowlers, who verily believed that the stumps were there to be hit, and he attacked them all the time, not waiting for the batsman to get himself out, but worrying him incessantly, seeking the chink in his armour.

Cook was a man of generous girth, and again like Harry Dean, really two bowlers in one. On a fast wicket, he bowled at a good medium pace, could swing the ball away from the bat, and whip down a faster ball without any obvious change in action. His away-swinger, bowled at good pace, with a low trajectory, spelled danger to the batsman in that it could not be easily distinguished from the straight ball or the break-back. When Cook bowled this ball, his arm dropped slightly, and the line of flight went obliquely to the off-stump. A batsman weak on the off-side could very well be caught in two minds, and have his off-stump taken or be snapped up at slip.

When there was rain about he would bowl a slowish off-break from round the wicket, but whether he was bowling his slow off-breaks or at medium pace, he bowled very few bad balls. 'Lol' Cook would have regarded a bad ball as a bank manager a bad debt, an error of judgement or a failure to apply the strict tenets of a long apprenticeship in his craft.

His best seasons were 1920 when he took 150 wickets for Lancashire at under 15 apiece, 1921 (148 at 22.9) and 1922 (142 at 19). In 1920 the list of his outstanding performances was remarkable indeed: 10 for 87 against Hampshire at Aigburth, 10 for 64 against Kent in Harry Dean's benefit match, 12 for 117 against Notts at Trent Bridge, 10 for 106 against Gloucestershire at Cheltenham, 10 for 67 against Sussex at Old Trafford, and most astonishing of all seven wickets for eight runs at Chesterfield when Derbyshire were put out for only 41.

'Lol' Cook and Harry Dean are the leading characters in a story, still told with relish by the older members at Old Trafford. In the Hampshire match at Aigburth in 1920, a game bedevilled by rain, Lancashire, who batted first, scored 182 and Hampshire replied with 174. In Lancashire's second innings Kennedy was almost unplayable. He took 9 wickets for 33 and Lancashire were put out for 57. Hampshire required only 66 to win, and on the second evening the night watchmen, Newman and Evans scored half a dozen runs without being separated.

On the third morning, after more overnight rain, there was bright sunshine. Harry Dean soon realized the likelihood of a sticky wicket later and that Lancashire's chances of winning depended on keeping the tail enders in whilst it remained easy.

He was heard to say to Cook as they walked out onto the field, 'Don't bowl 'em out, Lol.' For more than an hour they were happy to bowl a good length, without taking wickets. Evans made 21 and at one time Hampshire were within 12 runs of victory with half their wickets still standing.

Then Dean found that the wicket had become really sticky, and as they crossed between overs, he whispered to Cook, 'Now then, Lol'. The two bowlers launched their final assault. Hampshire lost their remaining wickets for only 10 runs and Lancashire gained a memorable victory by a single run. Though the story is told with a chortle to indicate the artfulness of two wily foxes, it illustrates too what confidence Harry Dean and 'Lol' Cook had in each other.

Both these cricketers were well liked and well respected at Old Trafford where they know a hard worker when they see one. If there is a bowler's heaven where hard work earns its fair reward, why then Harry Dean and 'Lol' Cook will come into their own at last.

XI

Cecil Parkin

Cecil Parkin was, for several seasons, 'Lol' Cook's partner in Lancashire's opening attack and he was also his opposite, the less direct, more subtle bowler who got the breaks and possibly more umpires to listen to him.

Compare their statistics for Lancashire. Figures can never tell the whole story, but these are significant:- Cook 821 wickets at 21 runs apiece in 13 playing seasons: Parkin 901 at 16 apiece in 9 playing seasons.

Parkin was the prince of diddlers and a joker to boot. He could do almost anything with a cricket ball, and like the alchemists of old who worked assiduously to find a formula to transmute base metals into gold, he was forever experimenting to produce the unplayable ball. Not content that his fast-medium deliveries were bringing him all the wickets and reward he deserved, he would practise his spinners on his long-suffering wife, who often finished these sessions with her finger nails black and blue, or reduced to tears by her husband's quickly breaking balls which she had not spotted in time.

Many a wife would have gone to the courts, no doubt, and sought a separation on grounds of physical and mental cruelty, but Cecil Parkin's good lady was made of sterner stuff and truer metal than most other spouses. She stuck nobly to her appointed rôle of dummy batsman, and Parkin would frequently say in after years that it was due to her encouragement that he had become the bowler he was.

Parkin would perform his experiments on the batsman in the middle, constantly ringing the changes, sometimes to the tune of six different balls in an over. When he was in this mood he was like a conjuror producing a strange assortment of articles from a hat. His captain must often have sympathized with the Iron Duke, all too aware that if Parkin were not frightening the opposition, he was certainly frightening him. For it was next to impossible to set a field for a man who was attempting to be every type of bowler in the same over, and Cecil Parkin was not exactly the sort of chap who would recognize it.

In the years between the two world wars, Maurice Tate was probably Parkin's only superior as a fast-medium bowler. Parkin was loose-limbed and had a fine action. He delivered the ball with his arm high and a full follow-through, he could spin it at whatever pace he was bowling and he could bring it back sharply from outside the off-stump.

Parkin's 'dolly mixtures', as some of his colleagues were wont to call them, utterly confounded the Yorkshire batsmen in the 'roses' match at Old Trafford in 1919. He took 14 wickets in this game, and his bowling and Harry Makepeace's batting were the main factors in a fine Lancashire victory. He cleverly changed his pace, flight and spin, and on this day with the bloom on the red rose he looked a really fine bowler.

Parkin was a native of County Durham, and as a young man he had played for Yorkshire before Lord Hawke (who was not a Yorkshireman by birth himself) discovered that he had first seen the light of day on the wrong side of the border. He first played for Lancashire in 1914 after a spell as professional with Church, the Lancashire League Club. In his first match, against Leicestershire at Aigburth, he took 14 wickets for 99 runs, and altogether in the six months he played that season he took 34 wickets. Unhappily the outbreak of war prevented the development of this early promise, and it was not until 1922 that Parkin was able to play regularly for the county again. An engagement with the Rochdale Club limited his first-class appearances to mid-week games.

Despite this limitation, he was picked to go to Australia in the winter of 1920-21 with J.W.H.T. Douglas's team. It was a disastrous tour and England lost all five Test matches. Parkin looked the best bowler in the side, but though he took many wickets it was often at considerable cost. He complained that he was given no opportunity to 'experiment' and that he was instructed to bowl outside the off-stump. For Cecil Parkin this must have been sheer torture. When he was discussing the tour in after years he would point out that he had taken 24 wickets in the matches against Queensland and South Australia when he had been able to bowl as he wished. This could have been a case of the Devil quoting statistics to his own advantage and choosing the best of them for his purpose, for Queensland and South Australia were not, at that time, notably strong sides. Australian cricketers and cricket writers, however, considered that Parkin was a better bowler than his figures suggested, and he had cause for consolation in that at least.

Parkin played for England in all five Tests of the 1921 home series against Australia, taking 16 wickets at a cost of 420 runs. In the Test at Old Trafford in July he took 5 wickets for 38 in Australia's innings, and he achieved the curious distinction, which he shared with R.G. Barlow, of opening both the batting and the bowling for England in the same match. (Barlow, however, was picked to do so; Parkin was not.) All chance of a positive finish had gone on the last day after H.L. Collins had effectively scotched any prospect England might have had of winning, by taking 5 hours to score 40 runs – an innings which Neville Cardus described as 'the scourge intolerable and the torturing hour'.

Possibly it was to recompense the spectators for the agonies they had endured during Collins's long tenancy of the crease, or more probably to emphasize the farcical situation to which the game had been reduced, that England's captain, the Hon. Lionel Tennyson sent in Parkin and Hallows to occupy as best they could the half-hour remaining for play. Evidently they gave the crowd some entertainment, for in that half hour 44 runs were scored, of which Parkin's share was 23.

This was the sort of situation Parkin revelled in. He was the supreme showman and the crowds loved it. He was really a much better batsman than he would admit, but he considered he was paid for bowling, not batting. In any event the spectators would much prefer to be cheered up by Cecil Parkin's travesty of batting than watch him show the recognized batsmen how to make their strokes. An innings by Parkin was a hilarious experience, and if it happened, as often it did, that Richard Tyldesley was the batsman at the other end, no comedy team then appearing on the halls or on the cinema screen could have caused more laughs.

He had a widespread repertoire of anecdotes, some true, some possibly not so true and some frankly apocryphal. He perfected the trick, seen more frequently today than in the days when Parkin played it, of bringing the ball from the ground to his hand with his foot, without having to stoop to do it.

I only saw Parkin play in his last season with Lancashire, the first summer that I watched cricket at Old Trafford. If I had been born two years earlier I might well have seen his wonderful performance with Richard Tyldesley at Headingley when they shot out the might of Yorkshire's batting for a paltry 33, after the Old Enemy had been set to score only 57 to win. More probably my father would not have bothered to travel across the Pennines in the circumstances, for a Yorkshire victory was considered a foregone conclusion, so much so that few people went down to the ground for the last rites.

The news of Yorkshire's humiliation spread like a prairie fire around the county, though at first it was received with stark incredulity. It was rumoured that more wives were beaten in Leeds that night for seemingly trivial reasons than for many years previously.

During the early years of the second World War, I saw Parkin umpiring in several charity matches. In his playing days he had never been an enthusiastic admirer of umpires and the cloak of authority ill-became him; he chatted incessantly to the batsmen, the bowlers, to anyone who was prepared to listen to him, and there were few who were not prepared to listen to Cecil Parkin.

His Test career, unfortunately, ended under a cloud, albeit a cloud that would be considered these days no bigger than a man's hand. Criticism of his captain, A.E.R. Gilligan under whom he had played in the Test series in South Africa in 1924, appeared in a newspaper article under his name. The article was, in fact, written by a 'ghost' writer, the curious name they give to the professional hack who helps cricketers and other sporting celebrities to clothe their thoughts in the right words. Who was the more responsible for the gaffe it was difficult to say with any degree of certainty. Parkin was noted for his full and frank comment, and very probably he had expressed the opinions mentioned in the article, but it seems injudicious, to say the least, of the writer to have put them into print. Be that as it may, the article had appeared under Parkin's name, and Parkin had to bear the responsibility. He never played for England again.

It is not generally known, I think, that a verse by Parkin appears in Leslie Frewin's anthology, 'The Poetry of Cricket'. It is short, appropriate and in limerick form:

'A bowler there was, name of Parkin,
Who had too much liking for larkin',

He made people stare,
And provoked a 'Lord's' prayer,
And he set all the little dogs barkin'.'

The 'little dogs', I suspect, were not all of the four-legged variety.

In his later years Parkin was licensee at an Old Trafford hostelry, not much more than half a mile from the ground where in his palmy days he had bowled his 'dolly mixtures' and joked and jested with his great contemporaries. There, of an evening, after a day at the cricket, he would entertain his friends and customers with his endless stories. When he died in 1943, his ashes, in accordance with his wishes, were scattered on the square at Old Trafford.

The irreverent – and be it remembered Parkin was one of their number – said that the scattering was a last request, typical of a cricketer who had bowled on those wickets and was well aware that dust was a plague to batsmen. One can imagine Cecil Parkin's infectious chuckle borne on the breeze from the Stretford end. He would have enjoyed that one immensely.

XII

Ernest Tyldesley

Ernest Tyldesley, sixteen years younger than his brother John played his first game for Lancashire in 1909 and his last in 1936. In the years between he scored more runs for the county at a better average than any other batsman – 34,222 at an average of 45. In all matches his run aggregate was close to 40,000.

His first appearance for the county side was against Warwickshire at Aigburth. He scored 61 and with Archie MacLaren took part in a stand which realized 128 runs in 90 minutes. Despite this early promise Ernest was slower to develop than Johnny. In 1913 he hit three centuries and in one remarkable week in June the two brothers each scored a century at Leicester and went on to the Oval where Johnny made 210 and Ernest 110. The performance of the Tyldesleys was not the only notable event of this game, for Tom Hayward became the second batsman after W.G. Grace to complete a hundred hundreds.

It was not, however, until cricket was resumed after the war that Ernest's batting ability was adequately revealed. His brother had coached him carefully, had the utmost faith in him, and with characteristic modesty, would frequently declare that Ernest was a better batsman than he was. I fancy that there would not be many people who saw them both at the full flowering of their talent, prepared unreservedly to support Johnny's contention. But the margin between them was slight; it was the margin between the great and the exceptionally good.

Ernest Tyldesley was a classical stylist, and inevitably in any discussion of his batting, the comparison arises between Johnny's methods and his own. Ernest had a range of strokes only a little less comprehensive than Johnny's, but his greatest strength was on the on-side. His hooking was magnificent and exhilarating to see, his driving and turning to fine-leg assured and elegant, his forcing of the straight ball wide of mid-on crisp and confident. Johnny was particularly strong on the off-side, but Ernest's off-side strokes came less naturally to him. I have seen it stated that Ernest could not cut. I can only assume that those who have said so, could not have seen him bat as frequently as I did.

Ernest was not as aggressive as Johnny, and he often looked an uncertain starter. It was, however, not so much initial uncertainty, as of deliberately refraining from making strokes until he had gauged the 'feel' of the wicket. When he was well set he could score quickly enough and he would make his strokes as to the manner born, for let it never be forgotten that Ernest Tyldesley learned his cricket in an age when batsmen were encouraged and indeed expected to parade their shots.

Possibly a change in the character of the wickets after the war of 1914-18 had much to do with the aggressive deficiency in Ernest's make-up. On the wickets of the nineteen-twenties there was generally no need to take risks to score runs. To the patient and the watchful batsman of sound technique they would come as surely and as naturally as the rising and the setting of the sun.

He did not play for England as often as his great ability warranted. He had the misfortune to be knocking on the door of the England side when there were such fine batsmen as Woolley, Hammond, Hendren, Mead, Holmes and Sandham competing with him for places. His Test match statistics certainly do not suggest that he was a failure on the occasions when he did play for his country. He played in 14 Tests and scored 990 runs, including three centuries at an average of 55. His brother Johnny played in 17 more Tests and scored nearly 700 more runs, but his average was 25 less than Ernest's. Of course in Johnny's day wickets were more unpredictable and runs had to be fought for much more vigorously.

Ernest's initial appearance for England was in the unhappy first Test against Warwick Armstrong's Australians at Trent Bridge in 1921, when Gregory and McDonald went on the rampage and put England out for 112 and 147, Australia winning the game by 10 wickets. Ernest was by no means the only England batsman to fail, and in the second innings he had the misfortune to be hit on the head by a ball from Gregory. He was knocked out and the ball rolled on to break the wicket.

The selectors panicked, made wholesale changes and still more changes after further defeats in the second and third Tests at Lord's and Leeds. Tyldesley was not given another chance until the fourth Test at Old Trafford, and he did enough there to give the selectors food for thought in that they had not persisted with him after the Trent Bridge débâcle. He played a magnificent undefeated innings of 78, hooking Gregory fearlessly. In the last Test at the Oval he scored 39, but had to wait five years for another chance.

In the fourth Test of the 1926 series, again at Old Trafford, he was brought back to the England team, almost by popular demand. He had made centuries that season in seven consecutive matches and scored over 1100 runs in nine games at an average of 141. He made top score for England (81), but was omitted from the side for the last Test at the Oval, a game which England won, and by winning it, took the 'Ashes' from Australia. Many people, particularly in Lancashire, were astonished that the England selectors had not persisted with him again. It was pointed out, in justification of the selectors' decision, that he had not timed Grimmett very well at Old Trafford, and had had no less than three 'lives' in the course of his innings.

On the 1927-28 tour of South Africa, he headed the English batting averages by a considerable margin, scoring more runs than Sutcliffe or Hammond. He had no failures in the Test matches, and scored elegant hundreds at Johannesburg and Durban.

The West Indies visited England in 1928, and Tyldesley scored 122 against them in the Lord's Test match. He went to Australia with A.P.F.Chapman's side in 1928-29, but in a party which included Hobbs, Sutcliffe, Hammond, Hendren, Jardine, Leyland and Mead, competition was again keen, and he played in only one Test scoring 31 and 21. On this tour M.A.Noble, the old Australian captain wrote of him: 'It seems a pity that, knowing this man to be a very fine batsman, the Englishmen did not persevere with him, regardless of a few early failures, until he struck form. They lost the services of a class batsman and great run-getter.'

We in Lancashire knew it of course, but sadly Ernest Tyldesley never played for England again. There is no doubt in my own mind that if the selectors had persisted with him, he would have established himself as a Test cricketer and would have been an asset to the England side.

For Lancashire his record has not yet been equalled. Of the 102 centuries he made during his career, 90 were made for the county. He hit five double-centuries, his highest score 256 not out against Warwickshire at Old Trafford in 1930. Twice he made a hundred in each innings of a county match – 165 and 123 not out against Essex at Leyton in 1921, and 109 and 108 not out against Glamorgan at Cardiff in 1930. Nineteen times he scored over a thousand runs in a season, three times over 2,000 and once over 3,000. In 1928 his total aggregate was 3024 at an average of 79.57.

It was in 1926 that in a remarkable sequence he scored 1477 runs in 13 innings between June 26th and August 6th:-

June 26, 28– 144 v Warwickshire at Birmingham
June 30. July 1, 2– 69 and 144 not out v Kent at Dover
July 3, 5, 6– 226 v Sussex at Old Trafford
July 10, 12, 13– 51 and 131 v Surrey at the Oval
July 14, 15, 16– 131 for Players v Gentlemen at Lord's
July 17, 19, 20– 106 v Essex at Nelson
July 21, 22, 23– 126 v Somerset at Taunton
July 24, 26, 27– 81 v Australia at Old Trafford (4th Test)
July 28, 29, 30– 44 v Essex at Leyton
July 31, Aug. 2, 3– 139 v Yorkshire at Old Trafford
Aug. 4, 5, 6– 85 v Middlesex at Old Trafford

Of all the fine innings that Ernest Tyldesley played for Lancashire, his double century at the Oval in 1923 will probably be remembered above the others. Lancashire were in a desperate position at the close of play on the second day, when with four wickets down they still needed 117 to escape an innings defeat. On the third morning Hitch bowling at tremendous pace posed the main threat to Lancashire's chances of survival. Tyldesley not only effectively removed him from the firing line, but thrashed impartially all the other Surrey bowlers, hooking, cutting and driving his way to 236 in five hours without giving a chance and the game was saved.

'Roses' matches are a good criterion of a Lancashire batsman's worth for Yorkshire notoriously begrudge conceding runs and centuries against them must be worked for and deserved. Ernest Tyldesley hit four hundreds in these games, a record only exceeded in 1967 when Pullar hit his fifth.

His twelve centuries in representative games included three Test hundreds and two for the Players against the Gentlemen at Lord's in 1926 and 1927.

Tyldesley was senior professional of the fine Lancashire side that won the County Championship three years in succession in 1926, 1927 and 1928, and as such he was one of the heroes of my boyhood. He never practised the ultra-cautious defensive technique that some other members of the championship side allowed to restrict their batting. His own defensive innings were dictated by conditions or circumstances rather than by the necessity to lay the foundations of an impregnable score.

In the field he was sound, sometimes brilliant, but in this department of the game, certainly, he never attained the standard of his brother.

He retired from active cricket in 1936, and in his later years he was elected to membership of the Committee of the county club. Honour was accorded to him, also from Lord's when M.C.C. decided to elect ex-professional cricketers to life membership and the name of Ernest Tyldesley was in the first list of players to be nominated.

In the last months of his life, his once keen eyesight failing and the legs that had carried him through twenty-four cricketing summers a constant source of pain, he could still shrug off his infirmities, for this splendid Lancastrian would never easily give best to anyone or anything.

My most enduring memories of his batting are of an innings of 165 at Headingley in 1927 when he put the Yorkshire bowling to the sword and took Lancashire to a first-innings lead, and a wonderful knock of 187 in Charles Hallows's benefit match at Old Trafford in 1928, when with Frank Watson he scored 371 for the second wicket against Surrey, still a Lancashire record.

It was all so long ago, but the enchantment lingers yet.

XIII

Harry Makepeace

Harry Makepeace served the Lancashire County Club for very many years, first as a player and afterwards as coach. He played his first game for Lancashire in 1906, his last in 1930. Between these years he played in 487 matches for the county, scoring over 25,000 runs at an average of 36. He hit 43 centuries, 42 of them in Lancashire matches, his highest score 203 at Worcester in 1923. In the same season he scored his only other double century – 200 not out against Northamptonshire at Aigburth – and altogether that summer he made over 2,000 runs in all matches.

Makepeace played in four Tests for England in Australia during the 1920-21 tour, and scored 279 runs, including a century in Melbourne at an average of 34.87. In a disastrous series, in which England lost all five Tests, he could hardly, therefore, be reckoned a failure.

Makepeace was not recognized as a bowler, and his bowling average for the county is considerably higher than his batting average, which seems to justify the lack of recognition of whatever bowling talent or pretensions he may have possessed. The records indicate, however, that during his first-class career he took 41 wickets, an average of less than two a season.

So much for the statistics. They reveal little of Makepeace, the man or even of Makepeace the cricketer. The gospel which Harry Makepeace preached and practised throughout his cricketing life was based first and foremost on sound defence. Makepeace had the soundest defence in the county cricket of his time. He was a terribly difficult batsman to get out, and that was not really surprising because his every stroke, his every thought, his every action at the wicket was dedicated to the proposition that come what may, he was there to stay. Many a poor bowler, toiling to outwit him, must have thought wryly that the old simile about his bat being broader than a barndoor was pitifully inadequate. It would, perhaps, have been more apposite to compare a barndoor with Harry Makepeace's bat than the other way round.

Makepeace was not a man for the frills or the fripperies. The famous dictum 'no fours before lunch on the first day of a "roses" match', has been variously ascribed to him or to Emmott Robinson. Who is the more likely to have said it? Surely the very words suggest the careful batsman rather than the canny bowler. On the criterion of probability I would plump for Harry Makepeace every time, though Emmott Robinson, who was wont to do his stint before lunch in these encounters would, one feels, have entirely supported the sentiment.

Yet for all his eschewing of the frills and fripperies, Makepeace was neither the unimaginative stone-waller nor an uninteresting batsman to watch. I saw him in my early days at Old Trafford when his playing career was drawing to its close. He had the ability, even then, to 'read' a ball early, as soon, or perhaps even before it had left the bowler's hand.

There was no back play by Makepeace to make the ball of shorter length, gaining that split second in time to make it more hittable. The left leg went firmly down the wicket, and Makepeace went forward, watching the ball carefully all the way. Harry Makepeace was the last batsman one could imagine making a speculative stroke. He was a vigilant batsman and his eye was keener than most. Therein lay the secret of his control.

For all his defensive-mindedness his technique was never merely utilitarian. His forward stroke was beautifully straight and in addition to his keen eye, his footwork was quick and sure. Before the ball reached him he was in a position to make his stroke and he could send the ball wherever he wished it to go, with little expenditure of effort or energy. He steered it in the direction he had earmarked for it when it left the bowler's hand. Not for Harry Makepeace the violent wastage of his energies which might have been required to set it on another course altogether.

His deftness of foot brought him an international soccer cap (like Jack Sharp he played with Everton) to add to the England cricket cap he won in the Australian summer of 1920-21. He did not play again for England, and doubtless the fact that 1921 was not one of his more successful seasons kept him out of the Test side that summer. Later, when his form returned, there was too keen a competition for places.

Towards the end of his playing career he was appointed

assistant coach at Old Trafford, and he subsequently became Chief Coach to the County Club. In his years of coaching he could be seen at the nets or with his youthful charges at the window of the young professionals' room in the pavilion, wearing his old cap, faded almost white by the sun of many summers. Harry Makepeace spent a lifetime in the service of Lancashire cricket, and the wisdom and ripe experience of that lifetime on the cricket fields were passed on devotedly and systematically to the youngsters who hoped, one day, to follow him in the county side.

It was sometimes said that Makepeace's coaching gave Lan- cashire cricket an excessively defensive outlook in the 'thirties which did not make the side popular visitors to cricket grounds up and down the country. But Harry Makepeace only taught what he had practised in his playing career – that a sound defensive technique is the essential foundation of good bats- manship. It was for the player himself to build on that foundation, and if Makepeace got the message through to his young men that the batsman's first duty is to stay at the wicket and do a good job for his side to the best of his ability and resources, there was nothing wrong in his teaching.

I last saw him at Weston-Super-Mare when Lancashire were festival visitors one year, and the holiday crowds were flocking into the ground to see Brian Statham in action. He was looking old and frail, and he seemed to be having some difficulty in persuading a gateman that he was, in fact, Harry Makepeace, and that he was with the Lancashire party.

Eventually he was rescued from his predicament by Colonel Green, his old captain, then the Lancashire President. It seemed terribly sad that in the evening of his days the gateman did not recognize him. But that gateman could not have seen him thrusting his left leg down the wicket at Old Trafford and executing that impeccably correct forward stroke.

'There is beauty in the bellow of the blast', wrote W.S. Gilbert in 'The Mikado'. If Harry Makepeace who wasn't one for frills and fripperies had been told that beauty could be associated with his cricket, he would have regarded it as something akin to heresy. None the less he left us much to remember.

XIV

Hallows and Watson

Hallows and Watson were once to me what Hornby and Barlow had been to Francis Thompson. They were the Lancashire openers of my boyhood, in the days when Harry Makepeace, the years mounting upon him, had slipped a little lower down the order.

Charles Hallows, who had first played for Lancashire in 1914 as a left arm bowler, played his last game for the county in 1932, but it was as a batsman and for a short time one of the best in England, that he made his mark in Lancashire cricket. In the intervening years he scored over 20,000 runs at an average not far short of 40. In that time he hit 55 hundreds (52 for Lancashire). His record includes three double centuries, and two occasions on which he made a century in each innings of a county match, curiously enough both away from Old Trafford.

For eleven seasons from 1919 to 1930 he exceeded a thousand runs, and in 1925, 1927 and 1928 he made over two thousand. In 1928, the best year of his cricketing career, he scored over 2,500 runs for Lancashire at an average of 65 and he achieved an honoured place in cricket records when he became one of the select group of three batsmen (Grace and Hammond were the others) who have scored a thousand runs in the month of May, as distinct from the distinguished but less select four others who have scored the thousand before the end of May. He went to his thousand in this remarkable sequence:-

100 against Northants, 101 and 51 not out against Glamorgan (all at Old Trafford), 123 and 101 not out against Warwickshire at Edgbaston, 22 against Middlesex at Lord's, 74 and 104 against Warwickshire at Nelson, 58 and 34 not out against Yorkshire at Sheffield and 232 against Sussex at Old Trafford.

When the Sussex match began at Old Trafford on May 30th, the Wednesday of Whitsun week, Hallows needed 232 to complete his thousand, and I imagine the prospect of attaining it was far from his mind. In the previous summer Hammond had performed the feat with three days to spare. Hallows had one innings or possibly two to make his runs. If it were one it required a double century, if two virtually a century in each innings, a formidable proposition, even for a batsman in the form of Hallows at that time.

He batted all through the first day and had scored 190 at close of play. He hit the remaining runs on the Thursday morning, the last day of the month, and he was caught from the very next ball he received after he had completed his thousand. I was at Old Trafford that day, and I remember very well the magnificent ovation Hallows received from the spectators and the cordial congratulations showered upon him by the Sussex players.

Hallows scored his runs at a better average (125) than Grace (112) or Hammond (74), but it should be mentioned that both Grace and Hammond had slightly higher aggregates than Hallows, and each reached their thousand in 22 days, whereas Hallows took 27 days to reach his.

In all Hallows hit eleven centuries that summer, but the full story of his services to Lancashire cricket is not told by his own record. Twelve times he and Watson shared in century-opening partnerships, and on five occasions they scored over 200 together. In the Glamorgan match at Old Trafford, after an opening stand of 202 in the first innings, they put on 107 in the second.

Sadly Hallows never reproduced the splendid form of that golden summer. He scored only half a dozen more hundreds between then and his retirement in 1932, though in the following season he achieved the distinction of carrying his bat through the Lancashire innings of the 'roses' match at Old Trafford. It was an innings of monumental patience which lasted seven hours.

Lancashire had lost their first three wickets for 14 runs, and another three middle-order batsmen could muster only another seven runs between them. Fortunately George Duckworth was in his most obdurate mood that day, and he helped Hallows put on 128 for the eighth wicket. Hallows finished with 152 not out, an innings that stemmed a collapse and saved the game.

For many summers, first with Harry Makepeace and then with Frank Watson, he opened the Lancashire innings, usually with the caution for which Lancashire cricket in the nineteen-twenties was well renowned. Sir Neville Cardus, in one of his absorbing volumes of autobiography, has described the opening of such an innings which happened to coincide with his own wedding morning.

He was reporting the game for the 'Manchester Guardian', and after seeing Makepeace and Hallows emerge from the pavilion gate, he left the ground to go into the city to meet his bride at the register office and complete the formalities in front of the registrar. When he returned to the ground to resume his coverage of the game, the two openers were still at the wicket, with less than 20 runs on the scoreboard.

Yet despite the slowness of their starting, and slowness here is a comparative term, for the slowness of those days was rarely as dilatory as some of the dreary crawls of modern times, you could be pretty sure that Hallows and Makepeace, or in later years Hallows and Watson, would have enough runs on the board at the fall of the first wicket to provide a solid foundation for the rest of the Lancashire innings. What is more, at the end of the day, the overall run-rate would indicate that not much time had been wasted.

It may seem curious to those who only knew Hallows in these moods that he was, by temperament, a much more aggressive batsman and that he adopted more cautious methods to suit the needs of his side at that time. He took his responsibilities as an opener very seriously, and when a solid foundation for an innings had been established and he felt able to revert back to his natural instincts, he could attack and punish the best bowling with savage ferocity. His favourite stroke was the straight drive to either side of the bowler, but he was especially strong on the on-side and he put a tremendous amount of power into his shots.

He was perhaps unfortunate to be chosen to play in only two Test matches, one against Australia in 1921 and the other against West Indies in 1928, but his two competitors for a place were Frank Woolley and Maurice Leyland, and he lacked the all-round ability of both these fine cricketers. In the field he was always dependable, but he was short of the speed essential to a fieldsman of the highest class.

Hallows was, however, a fine county batsman. He played a significant part in Lancashire's success in the three successive Championship wins of 1926, 1927 and 1928, and he will always be remembered for the trail of glory he blazed in that memorable summer when he scored his thousand runs in May.

In his later years, after a successful term as Chief Coach to the

Worcestershire County Club, during which they won the Championship, he returned to Old Trafford as Chief Coach. He could not command there the same success he had achieved at Worcester, but the young players he had under his charge in due time, under Jack Bond's captaincy, restored lost glories to Lancashire cricket after a long spell in the doldrums.

Frank Watson, Hallows's opening partner, and like him, a batsman who subordinated a basically aggressive temperament to the priorities of his side, played with the county for eighteen seasons. In that time he scored nearly 23,000 runs at an average of 37, and took 402 wickets at 31 runs apiece.

During his first-class career he hit 50 centuries, which included three double centuries and a treble century (made appropriately enough in his opening partner's benefit match). With Hallows he played a prominent part in Lancashire's Championship wins of 1926, 1927 and 1928. In 1930 when Hallows's star was waning and again in 1934 when Hallows had retired from first-class cricket, Lancashire were County Champions and Watson was a solid pillar of the batting. In 1928 he scored over 2,500 runs for the county at an average of 63. His nine centuries included his treble-hundred against Surrey at Old Trafford, two double centuries and a 'roses' century, also at Old Trafford.

Inevitably, when recalling Watson's cricket, one remembers the long sequences of lack-lustre innings, with strokes severely restricted so that the margin of error could be effectively reduced. But there were oases in the desert of drabness, innings that he played from time to time which allowed glimpses of the much more attractive batsman he could have been. One of these was his undefeated 300 in Hallows's benefit match, and another his 141 in Lancashire's second innings of the 'roses' match at Bradford in 1935, when a hundred of the runs were scored in boundaries. Lancashire had followed-on 172 behind after Bowes had wrecked their first innings, and Watson's innings was a magnificent gesture of defiance which, though it failed to save the game for Lancashire, showed a young batsman at the other end by the name of Washbrook that 'roses' cricket could produce something more than dour defensive play. Washbrook scored 85 himself that day, and the stand of the veteran and the youngster against the rampant Yorkshiremen was the brightest feature of a game that Lancashire might have been happier to forget than to remember.

Watson's philosophy, so long as he was opening for Lancashire, was to stay at the wicket and let the runs come, as in due time they would, and if the process was often dreary to watch it was also tremendously effective, for Lancashire in the twenties had no more acquisitive run-makers than Hallows and Watson. Frequently, when watching Watson at the wicket, one longed for some sign of fallibility, some hitting across the line of flight or the execution of a stroke with the bat at the wrong angle. Without any doubt at all his was one of the most difficult wickets in England to take, and any bowler who dismissed him early could be commended in despatches as having rendered meritorious service to his side. In the years of their employment as the foundation-builders of a Lancashire innings, the news that Hallows and Watson had been separated before their job had been satisfactorily achieved was greeted in the streets of Manchester with sad shakings of the head and gloomy prognostications of disaster around the corner.

Watson was a useful change bowler, and he could always be brought into the attack with the possibility of breaking up a stubborn partnership when all other resources had failed, or with the laudable objective of providing a rest period for one of the front-line bowlers who had done a fair stint.

He never achieved Test selection, though he toured the Caribbean with an M.C.C. side in the winter of 1925-26, and the records show that he scored a century against Jamaica at Kingston. It seems sad that Watson should have had no England cap to show for his years of solid work in county cricket, for he could no doubt have given backbone to many an England innings. Test matches in his day, however, were restricted to three or four days, and probably the selectors felt that the inclusion in a side of the doughty Watson would be to guarantee a draw before a ball had been bowled. If the Tests had been extended earlier to the modern span of five days, Frank Watson could possibly have become an England batsman as well as a good county player.

The consistent performances of Hallows and Watson as openers in Lancashire's Championship-winning years of the 'twenties spread tremendous confidence through the side. When Hallows's form deserted him after the summer of its full flowering, the famous partnership entered into its days of decline and at last it broke up.

Watson, who remained with the County Club until 1937 subsequently opened with other partners, but to me the start of a Lancashire innings was never quite the same. It was like having Gilbert without Sullivan, Laurel without Hardy, or Sankey without Moody, a sad example of the old order changing, yielding place to new.

XV

E.A. McDonald

Ted McDonald, one of my red roses who first bloomed far away
from Lancashire – in distant Tasmania, in point of fact – was the
finest fast bowler I ever saw, and I saw Larwood and Voce,
Farnes and Bowes, Lindwall and Miller, Statham, Trueman,
Tyson and Lillee. I would choose McDonald before all the others
for the several attributes, rarely present in one man, that go to
make up the perfect fast bowler.

He had, to start with, the lithe, lissom body of a wonderful
athlete, and if his rather angular colonial features have sometimes
been described as 'satanic', he had, too, a disarming smile that
effectively belied the unpleasant adjective. His run to the wicket
was beautiful to see. No earth-shaking thunder for him as for his
erstwhile Australian partner, Gregory. He was astonishingly
light on his feet, and he rippled to the wicket, his body perfectly
poised as a panther's, eyes, limbs and will, all supremely
co-ordinated and dedicated to the destruction of his prey.

So perfect was his action at the end of it that many observers
thought that he could not be as fast as other bowlers, who
seemed, in a flurry of limbs, to be putting more into it. They
were wrong. There are old cricketers still alive today who will
tell you that McDonald's fastest ball was faster than Gregory's.
He did not bump the ball at them as Gregory did with the ferocity
of a charging rhino, but bowled it well up and it came at them like
forked lightning, more often than not on the line of the
off-stump.

McDonald played in three Tests against J.W.H.T. Douglas's
team in the 1920-21 series in Australia, but he did not exactly set
the Antipodes on fire. It was a completely different story,
however, when he came to England with Warwick Armstrong's
side the following spring. From the first innings of the first game
at Leicester in which he took 8 wickets for 41 runs, it was
immediately obvious that here was a force with which the
English batsmen would have to reckon and subdue if they were

to have any hope at all of winning the 'Ashes'.

In the event, and with few exceptions, McDonald and Gregory struck such terror into their hearts that Australia began the series with a considerable built-in advantage, and finished it easy victors. Though Gregory was regarded as the more aggressive and dangerous of the two bowlers, the records show that it was McDonald who was the executioner in chief, Gregory the flamboyant henchman. In the series McDonald took 27 wickets for 668, average 24.74, Gregory 19 wickets for 552, average 29.

McDonald's Test career was limited by his engagement with Lancashire, and he did not play again for his country after that 1921 summer in England. For Lancashire, between 1924 and 1931, he took 1053 wickets at just under 21 runs apiece, and when one remembers that he was bowling for the whole of that time on easy-paced wickets, which gave him little assistance and from which very few bowlers of his day could extract much life, the measure of his achievement assumes even more heroic proportions.

In the era before 1914, Walter Brearley could always expect some help from the wicket, but in the 'twenties when McDonald bowled at Old Trafford, it was often only he who could make the ball rise above the height of the stumps. There is no doubt that if he had been able to bowl on pitches more suited to his pace, he would have taken many more wickets at considerably less cost.

It has been said that he never reproduced for Lancashire his blistering pace of the 1921 tour. It was hardly reasonable to expect him to maintain such a pace in six-day-a-week county cricket, for a Test fast bowler on tour is carefully nursed to prevent his bowling losing its edge. What is more widely agreed, however, is that McDonald was a better bowler of more varied accomplishments in his years with Lancashire if he were not quite so fast as in 1921.

Like the great fast bowlers of earlier days, he relied more on spin than on a persistent seam attack. Even when he was bowling quickly he could bring the ball back sharply, and he always had up his sleeve, awaiting the right moment, the ball of devastating, shattering pace.

His experience of League cricket with the Nelson Club stood him in good stead and added to his bowling education. He found that in damp conditions he could, by bowling round the wicket and turning the ball from the off at medium-pace, bowl as effectively and take as many wickets as with his faster deliveries on hard pitches. In Lancashire's Championship years, when the bowling never seemed varied or strong enough in depth to win the Chamionship, the part that McDonald played in his two rôles cannot be over-exaggerated.

He was always the bowler for the great occasion, or for the moment when his power and skill were most needed. 'Roses' matches brought the best out of him, and though Emmott Robinson might refer to him as 'The Taas-manian' in tones implying that Lancashire were playing a savage, Yorkshire cricketers had a genuine respect for him.

Lancashire's urgent quest for valuable Championship points in those years usually found McDonald ready and eager for the supreme extra effort when the needs of the side required it. There were times when games seemed destined for tame draws, until McDonald took them, as it were, by the scruff of the neck, and in an inspired spell of bowling, wrested victory from stalemate. In Lancashire's three successive Championship seasons, McDonald and Richard Tyldesley between them took 847 wickets – McDonald 515, Tyldesley 332. The decisive part the two bowlers played in the winning of the Championship is well illustrated by these figures.

McDonald first played for Lancashire in 1924, but he was not fully available and the summer was depressingly wet, circumstances which prevented his achieving his maximum effectiveness. In 1925, however, he was available throughout the season, and he took 182 wickets in Championship games, 205 in all matches at slightly over 18 runs each. His haul from Surrey in the two games that season was 20, he took 11 Leicester wickets at Old Trafford and ten in the return game, ten Glamorgan wickets at Swansea and another ten (including a 'hat-trick') at Brighton. In the Somerset match at Old Trafford which was finished in a single day McDonald played a prominent part with both bat and ball.

In 1926, the first of the three Championship years, McDonald's wickets numbered 175 in county matches at 20 runs apiece (including another 'hat-trick' against Kent at Dover) and he distinguished himself in the Middlesex game at Old Trafford with a hard-hit undefeated hundred, his only century in first-class cricket.

He utilised spin much more on the wet pitches of the following season, and took 150 wickets that summer, his best performances 8 for 73 and twelve in the match at Northampton.

McDonald's best season was in 1928, when at thirty-six years of age, he played in all the thirty Championship games and maintained his form and speed magnificently to take 178 wickets (190 in all matches) at 19 runs apiece. He had 11 for 113 against Essex at Colchester and in a remarkable sequence of four matches, all won by Lancashire, he took, in the course of a fortnight 35 wickets for 526 runs, bowling with tremendous spirit and dedication, though he was required to work for long spells.

It was in the Kent match at Old Trafford that McDonald's superb bowling was seen at its best. Kent had batted first and with Woolley, in his most scintillating form, their score stood at 262 for 4. He and Ames had put on 128 for the third wicket, treating all the Lancashire bowlers, McDonald not excepted, with scant respect. Then McDonald struck. Ames was hit on the wrist by a ball that rose viciously; the next ball saw his middle stump removed clean from its resting place.

Bryan helped Woolley add another 91 for the fourth wicket but Woolley's fine knock was ended when at 151 he hit McDonald to leg and Iddon held a splendid catch. That was virtually the end for Kent. McDonald and Sibbles gobbled up the last six wickets for 15 runs, McDonald finishing with 7 for 101.

The Lancashire batsmen, doubtless inspired by McDonald's spirited performance, replied with 478 for 5 and the innings was declared after an hour's batting on the last morning. The rest of the game belonged almost exclusively to McDonald. Bowling unchanged, with furious pace and fire, he shot through the Kent batting to take another 8 wickets for 53 to make his match record 15 for 154. Again it was Woolley who provided the main resistance; again it was McDonald who induced him to cut at a tempting out-swinger so that he was taken exultantly at second slip.

This was the very stuff of cricket, a great batsman opposed to a superb bowler and no quarter given. I who was privileged to see it all with the ecstatic eye of boyhood will carry that duel in the memory whilst memory itself lasts.

Had we but known it that wonderful summer, the great fire that was Ted McDonald was never to burn so brightly again. At

ROY TATTERSALL
(L.C.C.C./News Chronicle)

ERNEST TYLDESLEY
(L.C.C.C.)

R.H. SPOONER
(L.C.C.C.)

WALTER BREARLEY
(L.C.C.C.)

JOHNNY BRIGGS
(L.C.C.C.)

BRIAN STATHAM
(*L.C.C.C./News Chronicle*)

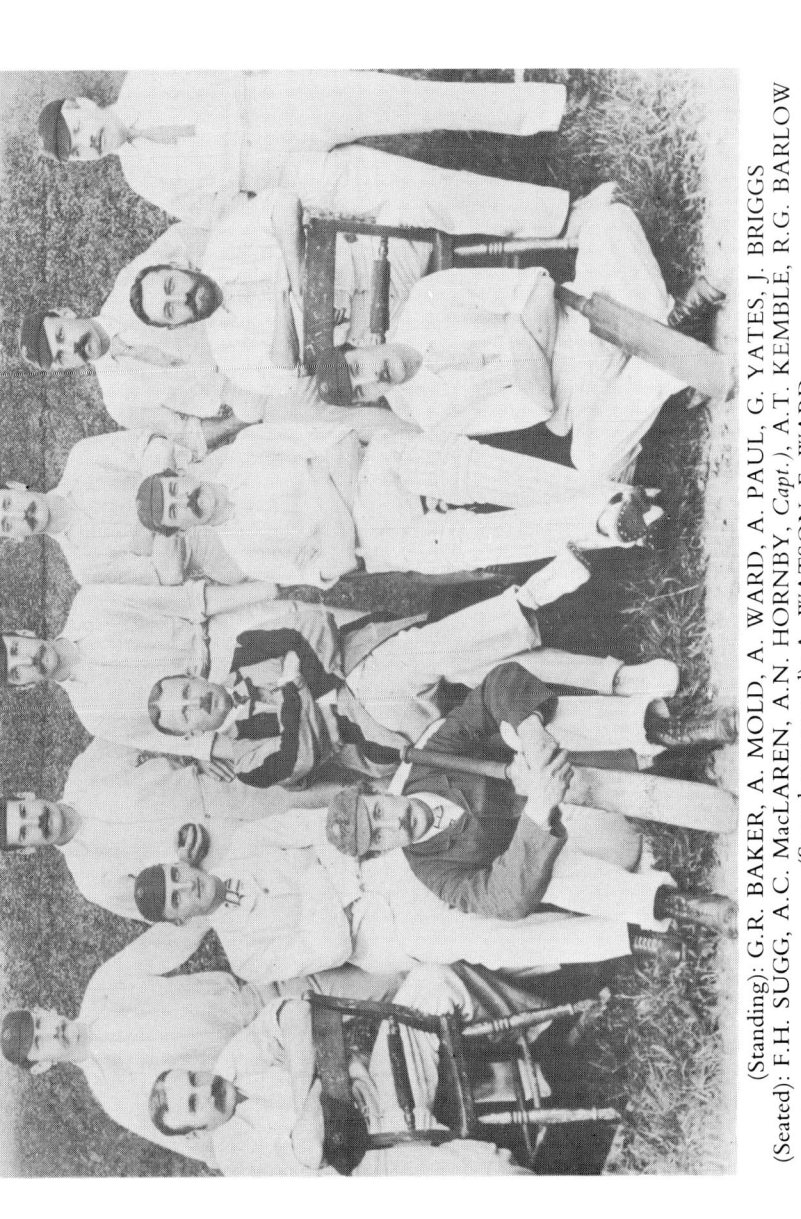

(Standing): G.R. BAKER, A. MOLD, A. WARD, A. PAUL, G. YATES, J. BRIGGS
(Seated): F.H. SUGG, A.C. MacLAREN, A.N. HORNBY, *Capt.*), A.T. KEMBLE, R.G. BARLOW
(Seated on ground): A. WATSON, F. WARD
Lancashire C.C.C., 1890

(Lancashire C.C.C.)

HARRY MAKEPEACE rings-in a new season
(L.C.C.C./Daily Graphic)

(Standing): H. RYLANCE, (*Sec.*), L. COOK, C. HALLOWS, R. TYLDESLEY, E. TYLDESLEY,
C. PARKIN, J. TYLDESLEY, HEAP
(Seated): H. MAKEPEACE, R.H. SPOONER, J. SHARP, (*Capt.*), F. MUSSON, H. DEAN
Lancashire C.C.C., 1920
(Manchester Evening News)

CLIVE LLOYD
(Action Agency)

thirty-six his remaining years as a fast bowler were obviously limited; even he, lion-hearted as he was, could not go on for ever. In 1929 he took 140 wickets, in 1930, 108 (including the third 'hat-trick' of his first-class career at Edgbaston, and to his own great delight the wicket of Don Bradman at Aigburth). The cost, however, was increasing, and in 1931 he played in only 14 matches, before his contract, which had a further year to run, was terminated by mutual consent and he returned to league cricket. McDonald was tragically killed in a motoring accident in 1937. He had stopped his own car, and was walking back along the road to offer assistance to the victims of a collision, when he was struck down by another car. The manner of his dying was typical of the man. Where he was needed, there would he be, were it to give aid or comfort to those who required it, or at Old Trafford, moving rhythmically and silently to the wicket over the velvet grass, the breeze at his back and his shirt billowing in it, bowling his heart out for his adopted county.

Like a brilliant comet he blazed across the Lancashire sky for only six full seasons and two shortened ones, and then was seen no more. But whilst the blaze lasted the light it gave was bright indeed, and the memory of it will always be sweet.

XVI

Richard Tyldesley

In marked contrast to the lean athleticism and mahogany-complexioned colonial features of Ted McDonald, Richard Tyldesley was a rotund Falstaffian figure with a countenance like a rosy apple. He was a product of the good Lancashire earth, raised in Westhoughton, a town in the industrial hinterland between Bolton and Wigan where they are as knowledgeable about their cricket as about their whippets and their pigeons.

He was no relation to Johnny and Ernest Tyldesley, but three of his family had played for the county before the first World War. Billy, a left-handed batsman, who first played in 1908, was killed in the last year of the war; James, who at one time looked capable of developing into a fine fast bowler was probably defeated in the transition from usefulness to excellence by the loss of the war seasons, and Harry, a third brother, played in a few matches, but never settled into the side.

Richard was supposed to be a leg-break and googly bowler, but he was a bit of a 'diddler' also, and he took a lot of his wickets with a ball that did not break at all. His top-spinner, a ball which went straight through after pitching and which he bowled with prodigious finger-spin, brought him many victims, a large proportion of them from l.b.w. decisions. He did not turn the ball very much, but just enough to beat the bat, and he was sufficently quick to make it difficult for batsmen to move to the pitch of the ball.

It was sometimes said that Tyldesley took more wickets than he deserved simply because batsmen would not use their feet to play him. The superficial judgement was less than just to him. If it had been said that too many batsmen could not use their feet, it would have been nearer the mark. Dick's greatest asset was his consistency of length, which he seemed able to maintain, even when he was being subjected to heavy punishment.

Only batsmen of the keenest eye and quickest footwork could move out to him, but he was more than a match for most county batsmen, particularly if the wicket were giving him any help at all. Even on the easy-paced wickets of the nineteen-twenties his record was impressive as his figures for Lancashire from 1922 to 1931 show:

	WICKETS	AVERAGE
1922	100	17.89
1923	133	15.28
1924	167	13.32
1925	137	15.10
1926	128	16.86
1927	100	20.02
1928	104	19.06
1929	154	15.57
1930	133	15.25
1931	116	15.97

Dick Tyldesley first played for the county side in 1919 and in the thirteen seasons between then and 1931 he took 1449 wickets for Lancashire at 16.65 runs each. Until the arrival of Brian Statham on the cricketing scene, his aggregate of wickets had been exceeded only by Briggs and Mold.

Tyldesley's immense usefulness to Lancashire did not end with the number of wickets he took himself. His captain could always rely on his consistent accuracy to shut up an end for an hour or two hours, either as support or relief for Parkin or McDonald as the occasion demanded. Over after over he would bowl, his ruddy face wreathed in honest sweat, hitching up his flannels as he walked to his bowling mark, a habit rather than a necessity, for his generous girth precluded any likelihood of their slipping.

Dick Tyldesley rarely wore a cap and seemed almost to have an antipathy to them, particularly to the rather gaudily-coloured college caps which the young amateurs used to sport in the University matches or during the vacations when they played for their county sides. Whether these patrician caps offended his staunchly plebeian sympathies, or whether he recognized in the wearers the possibilities of a few cheap wickets to boost his average, there is no denying that the very sight of them had the same effect on him as a red cloak to a bull. If he were not bowling as he beheld one coming through the pavilion gate, he would chafe restlessly until he could get at 'the scholar with the fancy

cap', and not infrequently he would indicate to his captain that
these gentry were his legitimate prey. Wise was the captain who
did not wait to be told.

Tyldesley's most successful season was in 1924 when he took
184 wickets in all matches at under 14 runs apiece. The story of
the destruction of Yorkshire with Cecil Parkin at Headingley has
already been told. He took seven of Glamorgan's wickets at
Aigburth, eleven against Surrey at Old Trafford, eleven at
Leyton and twelve against the South African tourists.

When Leicestershire came to Old Trafford he took five
wickets without conceding a run, and at Aigburth the following
month he had this remarkable analysis against Northamptonshire.

Overs	Maidens	Runs	Wkts.
14	12	6	7

He and Parkin bowled unchanged in both innings against
Warwickshire and shared the wickets between them.

Tyldesley played a valuable part in Lancashire's Cham-
pionships of 1926, 1927 and 1928, and in 1929 he had another
remarkable season, heading the first-class bowling averages, and
three times taking more than ten wickets in a match. At Derby he
performed the considerable feat of taking four Derbyshire
wickets in four balls.

In 1930 he helped Lancashire to yet another Championship
win, and his bowling won him a Test place against Australia at
Trent Bridge, an appearance which caused him to miss his own
benefit match.

Sadly, at the end of the 1931 season, a disagreement over future
terms took Tyldesley away from Old Trafford, and he was lost
to county cricket at the age of 33 when he still had several more
seasons of usefulness to Lancashire in him.

As a batsman he was inclined much more towards the rustic
than the academic; many a Lancashire innings, begun and
continued in sober decorum, was enlivened in its later stages by
the agricultural flourishes of Dick Tyldesley.

In the field he was a very good close-to-the-wicket fieldsman,
and despite his considerable girth, he made many fine catches at
slip, frequently from the bowling of McDonald.

His Test career was not particularly successful: in seven

appearances – three against Australia and four against South Africa – he took 19 wickets but at a cost of 32 runs each. The cynics said that he was out of his class; I prefer to think that he did not do himself justice.

Dick is remembered at Old Trafford with much affection, and from the pavilion photographs of the Championship-winning teams of which he was a member, his amiable round face looks out for all time on the field of the great triumphs of his cricketing years.

XVII

George Duckworth

A good wicket keeper is a priceless asset to any cricket team, a wonderful encouragement to bowlers and fieldsmen alike.

George Duckworth kept wicket in the golden years of Lancashire's Championship successes, and helped McDonald and Richard Tyldesley to many of their wickets. At one time he was keeping wicket to McDonald for Lancashire and to Larwood for England, two of the greatest fast bowlers of that or any other time.

Duckworth was Lancastrian to the core, born in Warrington and educated at the local Grammar School. He first played for the county in 1923, and at once became Lancashire's regular wicket-keeper, holding the place for fifteen seasons until his retirement from regular first-class cricket at the end of the 1937 season. Subsequently he made three further appearances, the last in a festival game at Harrogate in 1947.

In his first-class career, in all matches, he claimed 1094 victims (754 caught, 340 stumped). For Lancashire, in 424 matches he had 921 victims (634 caught, 287 stumped). His total of 107 dismissals in 1928 is a record for a Lancashire wicket-keeper in one season. He played for England in 24 Test matches, ten against Australia, and achieved 60 dismissals (45 caught, 15 stumped).

Duckworth succeeded Strudwick as England's wicket-keeper, and he kept Ames, who was a much better batsman, out of the England side until Ames was required for his batting. It was then decided that the policy of playing two wicket-keepers and using only one should not be continued, though in point of fact Ames was capable of fielding in any position.

At his best Duckworth was a neater, more efficient wicket-keeper than Ames, and if the England Test side gained in batting strength when Duckworth left it, the wicket-keeping never regained the outstanding quality of the Lancastrian's finest years.

Duckworth had a tremendous zest for cricket which he carried into his retirement, for when he took off his pads for the last time, he was by no means lost to the game. In fact he began a new career as a radio and television commentator, and, it should be added, a very knowledgeable one. His ability to read a game, a valuable legacy from his playing days, helped many listeners and viewers, not fully acquainted with the finer points, to a quick and shrewder appreciation of the issues involved.

It seemed that he could never get enough cricket, though he had many other interests – Rugby League football was one of them as a reporter and commentator – and he acted as baggage master on several M.C.C. overseas tours, and for several sides touring England.

On Duckworth's first visit to Australia in 1928-29, M.A. Noble said of him, 'he bustles along between overs as eager to continue the strife as a boy is to ride his first bicycle, and his youthfulness and enthusiasm appeal to the crowd'.

He was noted for his shrill appeals, and it used to be said of him in Australia that when he appealed for a decision in Sydney, an umpire was liable to give a batsman out in Melbourne. But he never appealed for appealing's sake, and when he did you could be sure that there would be no frivolity about it and no thought of badgering an umpire into a favourable decision. On the contrary, Duckworth only appealed if he was absolutely convinced of the justice of his cause, and his loud plea for official endorsement of his own opinion was as much a call to High Heaven that the umpire should be made to see the light. It was his job to see the batsman out, but fairly out, in the shortest possible time and all his powers of body, mind and spirit were directed to that end.

He was not an unobtrusive wicket-keeper in the manner of Oldfield of Australia, his great contemporary, of whom it was said that a batsman was too often unaware of his presence until the bails were whipped off or there was an almost apologetic appeal for a catch at the wicket. A batsman was always well aware of Duckworth's presence, for he was rarely still and he expended a tremendous amount of energy in the course of an innings.

He was amazingly quick, and he could whip across to take near-impossible catches from glances to the leg-side off McDonald which altered the course of many a game in the nineteen-twenties. His hands were as safe as any that have kept wicket in any country at any time, and his clean taking of the ball was an object lesson of the wicket-keeper's art. He had, of course, the marked advantage of having kept wicket to the fast bowling of McDonald for his county and of Larwood for England. To both these bowlers he would stand well back, to a distance where he could take catches without getting in the way of first-slip.

A keen and enthusiastic wicket-keeper can raise prodigiously the fielding performance of a team, and in this department Lancashire had much cause to be grateful for the effect of Duckworth's influence. He loved to have the ball hurled back at him from the field, even where there was no possibility of a run-out, and if a young player was inclined to be a little lethargic in his returns, you could be pretty sure that a fatherly word from Duckworth the next time they were in close proximity would be the prelude to some extra zip and zest.

He was forever stressing the importance of keenness and dedication in the field, and it was typical of him that when the young Washbrook went to his first Test match, Duckworth advised him not to worry overmuch about his batting, but to make sure there were no complaints about his fielding. A team's fielding is the hallmark of its efficiency as a unit, and Duckworth, who possessed a shrewd mind as well as a cheerful countenance, was concerned at all times to see that that efficiency was maintained.

He had his off-days, of course, as we poor mortals must all have in this imperfect world. At the Oval in the fifth Test match with Australia in 1930, fate or fortune, call it what you will, played cruel sport with him. He missed Woodfull at 6, Ponsford at 23 and 45 and Bradman at 82. Woodfull went on to score 54, Ponsford 110 and Bradman 232, so it was argued that Duckworth's lapses cost England as many as 285 runs and the opportunity of winning, or at least squaring the series. The argument may be academic, but whatever the rights or wrongs of it, there can be no doubt that Duckworth himself would be the least philosophic about it. The torment for him would lie as much in the knowledge that he had slipped, however temporarily, from his own high standards, as that he had let England down in a Test match.

Duckworth's batting was as perky as the man himself, but in the blistering cauldron of 'roses' cricket, he could be as dour and immovable as any of his colleagues if the chips were down and Yorkshire tails were up. Then Emmott Robinson and his rampaging confederates would soon discover that George Duckworth was not prepared to surrender his wicket lightly. The sights and sounds of cricket are part of the delectable remembrances of a lifetime's love of the game, and if, in writing earlier of McDonald, I recalled with nostalgic reminiscence the sight of his supple figure running silently and menacingly to the wicket, the picture would need for completeness the aggressive little figure of Duckworth, crouched beyond the stumps at the other end, ready to take off in any direction for the snick he knew must come.

It is an Elysian scene, and if in after time, there is an Elysium where the great cricketers foregather, I am certain that that reputed abode of quiet and peace will not be so quiet and peaceful whilst George Duckworth is about.

XVIII

Jack Iddon

Jack Iddon, a right-hand batsman and left-arm spin bowler, played for Lancashire from 1924 until 1945, except for the years of the second World War when no cricket was possible. He was a highly-valued member of five Championship-winning teams, and for many years he batted at No.4 in the county side, immediately after Ernest Tyldesley.

His career figures are impressive. For Lancashire he scored nearly 22,000 runs at an average of 37 and took 533 wickets at 26 runs apiece. He hit 46 centuries, including four double centuries, and in fact, he scored hundreds against every other county, a record not shared by some who were considered greater batsmen than he. His best season as a batsman was in 1934 when he scored nearly 2,400 runs at an average of 53, and with the ball in 1932 when his 80 wickets cost him 17 runs apiece.

For some time, in his early days with Lancashire, Iddon had been regarded as possibly the long-awaited and long-sought successor to Johnny Briggs as a left-arm spinner, but he would have been the first to admit that he was not in the same class as little Johnny, and in point of fact he was too good a batsman to practise the concentration required of a great bowler.

Iddon commanded a fine range of strokes, and when he chose to put them on view, there were few more stylish batsmen in cricket. Unfortunately, in the days of his prime Lancashire cricket was dedicated more to utility than to beauty and his style was too frequently sacrificed to the overall strategy of the side.

The stroke one remembers most when Iddon's name is mentioned is his straight drive, a stroke of peerless authenticity, executed like the cracking of a whip, the body beautifully upright, eyes following the ball on its almost inevitable course to the boundary fence, the whole bearing of the man exuding a rightful pride that this shot was his and his alone.

Jack Iddon was a handsome man, and an impeccably turned out one. His dark, aquiline features embodied the fashionable good looks of his day, and they fluttered more feminine hearts at Old Trafford in the early days of the talking picture than did some of the black and white images of the Hollywood matinée idols on the cinema screens. He was one of the most dapper cricketers I have ever seen. From the boundary's rim I would often admire the beautiful cut and crease of his flannels, the spotless, billowing whiteness of his shirt, the trim neatness of his boots, the cleanness of his cap and the eternal redness of the rose cresting it. Iddon had the body of an athlete, muscles of whipcord, wrists of steel. His returns from the outfield to George Duckworth were delivered with a seemingly effortless flick of the wrist and Duckworth would take them in his gloves just above the stumps.

'Roses' games seemed to bring the best out of him, and I remember particularly a wonderfully defiant innings of 142 not out at Old Trafford in 1934 when the Yorkshire bowlers were on the rampage, and a match-winning bowling performance at Sheffield in 1937 when he took 9 wickets for 42 in Yorkshire's second innings.

Apart from these brushes with the 'Old Enemy' I recall with particular pleasure two fine undefeated double centuries, both at Old Trafford – 200 against Notts in 1934, one of his six centuries that season, and 217 against Worcestershire in 1939 when the war clouds were lowering over Europe and that summer's cricket was the last we were to see of the first-class game for five years.

When the war was over Iddon was 42 years of age. He had decided to play in the 1946 season as an amateur, and it is possible that he might have captained the county side, bringing to it experience that would have been extremely valuable at that difficult period, but this was not to be. Before the season began he was tragically killed in a motoring accident and another fine cricketer was lost to the game he had adorned.

Iddon played for England five times in the 1935 home series with South Africa, scoring 170 runs in 6 innings, highest score 73, a record hardly calculated to set the world ablaze, but at an average of nearly 30 by no means that of a failure.

In the early nineteen thirties he was cricket coach at the school I attended, and when Lancashire were playing at Old Trafford he would come over from the ground in the evening to put us through our paces. He told me that I was holding my bat wrongly, and showed me the correct way. Unfortunately I cannot say that the new grip improved either my technique or my scores, but I can say that the advice he gave me about my bowling improved it immeasurably and my wicket-taking increased most encouragingly.

For this and for all the pleasures his cricket gave me over the years, I have good reason to be grateful to Jack Iddon.

XIX

Eddie Paynter

In the years immediately preceding the outbreak of the second World War, Lancashire's batting and indeed much of Lancashire's cricket was dominated by Eddie Paynter and Cyril Washbrook. As opening partners they set many a Lancashire innings on the right road. Both were prolific scorers, and the wonderful understanding they achieved in their running between the wickets must have convinced Francis Thompson, had he been able to see them, that as run-stealers Hornby and Barlow were hardly in the same class.

Paynter's cricketing career was remarkable in that he was 28 years of age before he played his first game in the county side, and he had six seasons to wait before the chance came. Lancashire, in those days, had a powerful batting side, and even though he played in half the matches in the summer of 1930, he was in some doubt at the end of the season whether or not he could retain his place, so much so that he decided to leave Old Trafford and try his hand at league cricket.

Before the new season opened he had changed his mind, and it was well for Lancashire and England cricket that he did so. In that season he opened England's innings at Old Trafford with Herbert Sutcliffe. He scored only 3 on that occasion, but that was the first of 20 appearances for England.

It is fair to say that but for the war Paynter would have gained many more than 20 caps, for the tragedy about the career of this wonderful little cricketer was that six years were lost at the beginning and six at the end of it. His first-class cricket was compressed into ten seasons, and his record is the more remarkable for the shortness of the span.

For Lancashire he scored over 16,000 runs at an average of 41. His Test record is even more impressive – 1540 runs in the twenty matches at an average of 59. Only Herbert Sutcliffe has a better average for England. But it was against Australia that

Paynter excelled. Among English batsmen his name, like that of Abou Ben Adhem, leads all the rest – his average 84·42. Only Bradman, if one includes Australians as well as Englishmen in Tests between the two countries betters this. His average was 89·78.

Paynter made his Test début against Australia in the controversial and acrimonious 'body-line' tour of 1932-33, and he won fame with a performance in the fourth Test of that series at Brisbane for which his name will always be remembered as long as the history of cricket is recorded. During the game he developed tonsillitis and was very properly put to bed in hospital with a temperature of 102. Australia had batted first and had made 356. On the Saturday evening England had scored 99 without losing a wicket, and there was a reasonable chance that Paynter would not be required to bat until the Tuesday.

On Monday, however, wickets began to tumble, and shortly after tea when the sixth wicket fell, Paynter walked slowly down the pavilion steps, looking pale and ill. He had been listening to the commentary on the game on his bedside radio, and contrary to the instructions of the doctors and the nursing staff he left the hospital, clad only in pyjamas and dressing gown and hastened to the ground by taxi.

The sun was cruelly hot at that time of the day, and only Paynter himself knew what an ordeal he endured, though he would have been the last to reveal it. The Australian crowd realized it all right. Above all other qualities in a man the Australians admire guts, and Eddie Paynter won an enduring place in the hearts of that crowd by his innings that day. Remember that this was a tour which produced ill-feeling and dissension between the sides and Englishmen were not exactly popular in Australia that summer. Yet Paynter at the end of the tour was the most popular and best respected member of the M.C.C. side.

The story of his innings has been told often enough, but it will bear retelling in a record of Lancashire cricket and cricketers. For four hours he defied the Australian attack, scored 83 himself and with Hedley Verity, his opponent in many a 'roses' battle in England, he put on 96 in a stand which completely transformed the course of the game. They were still together when Australia's total was passed, and though England's first innings lead was inconsiderable, the moral advantage they had wrested from the

Australians was not.

When Australia batted a second time Woodfull, Richardson, Ponsford and Bradman were all out for 108, and their hopes rested on McCabe and the two left-handers, Darling and Bromley, who had been brought into the side in the belief that they could counter fast leg-theory. That belief, however sincere it might have been, proved ill-founded, the remainder of the batting crumbled and England were left to score 160 to win the match and the 'Ashes'.

Sutcliffe was dismissed early, but Jardine and Leyland saw England safely through, and appropriately it was Paynter who made the winning hit – a six. Then he went back to bed.

There is perhaps some excuse for the failure of the Lancashire authorities to recognize Paynter's worth during his earlier days at Old Trafford for the county side in those days included such famous batting names as Ernest Tyldesley, Makepeace, Hallows, Watson and Iddon. Who could have considered dropping any one of these, at the height of his powers, in favour of an unestablished stripling, however promising his talent? Knowing what we now know, it seems reasonably certain that the earlier inclusion of Paynter would have brought to the Lancashire teams of the late 'twenties a belligerent brilliance which was the one ingredient those admittedly fine sides conspicuously lacked.

There was less excuse for the England selectors who left him out of the team which toured Australia in the winter of 1936-37. He had not enjoyed, comparatively speaking, one of his more successful seasons in 1936; doubtless the selectors were influenced by this fact into deciding that he was not in form, and that his inclusion in the team would involve too great a risk of his not finding it. It was an error of judgement to which all mortals are prone from time to time, but none the less regrettable for that. In the event, England lost the 'Ashes' after winning the first two Tests of the series.

Whether Paynter's availability would have swung the series England's way is now a hypothetical speculation. What is certain is that the sight of those green Australian caps always brought out the best in Eddie Paynter.

In the 1938 series in England – the series of Hutton's record score of 364 at the Oval – he was second only to Hutton in the England batting averages. Both had averages over 100; Hutton's was slightly better, but in the Oval game Hutton made his record score; Paynter made a 'duck'.

At Trent Bridge in the first test of that summer, Paynter scored 216 not out of an England total of 658, after Hutton and Barnett had put on 219 for the first wicket. Hutton, Barnett and Compton all made hundreds, and in such a welter of runs, on a perfect batting wicket, one might have reckoned Paynter's double century no more than the inevitable plundering of a tired and dispirited attack. Against all that had gone before or followed, however, it stood out as a brilliant exhibition of sustained aggression.

In the second Test at Lord's, after three wickets had fallen cheaply, Hammond and Paynter came together and rescued the England innings with a fourth wicket stand of 222. This time it was Hammond who scored the double century; Paynter was unlucky to miss his own hundred by a single run, but his exemplary behaviour at yet another time of crisis in England's fortunes underlined the shortsightedness of the selectors who had decided not to send him to Australia the previous winter.

McCormick had shot out Hutton, Edrich and Barnett for 31 when Paynter joined Hammond, and together they proceeded to reconstruct the innings from the wreckage of the early batting. Hammond bludgeoned the rampant McCormick out of the attack whilst Paynter turned his attention and his aggression on Fleetwood-Smith. Both batsmen heaped upon the venerable head of O'Reilly indignities such as that great bowler rarely suffered.

But Paynter's part in the match was by no means finished. Though England led on the first innings McCormick again achieved a quick break-through in the second, and at one time five wickets were down for 76. Then Compton and Paynter came together, and in a defiant partnership they carried England safely away from the prospect of defeat. Paynter's share was 43, but this time it was the stubborn Paynter rather than the aggressor that was on view. The effect was the same; once again Eddie Paynter had shown that there was no better man than he to have on hand in a crisis.

Still his part was not yet done. Ames had injured a finger, and could not keep wicket in Australia's second innings. Who volunteered to put on the gloves in his place? Who but Eddie Paynter. His performance was extremely creditable, and he caught Barnett, the Australian wicket-keeper with such professional aplomb that Barnett, had he been well versed in the works of the Bard of Avon, must surely have recognized as did Shylock the Jew, a very Daniel come to judgement.

Paynter's innings in the last Test (Hutton's Test) was in the nature of anti-climax. He came to the wicket late on the Monday afternoon with England's score at 546 for 3. Since the Saturday morning, during the hours of play, he had been putting on, sitting in and taking off his pads, ready for the call which had not come until that moment. His innings in the Trent Bridge and Lord's Tests had prepared the crowd for some further scientific slaughter of the perspiring Australian bowlers, and his brisk, purposeful walk as he strode to the wicket certainly suggested that Paynter himself might have had the same idea in mind. Whether he had or not, the truth is that he was out leg-before-wicket without scoring.

He consoled himself, I imagine, with the thought that at last he could take his pads off and keep them off. Certainly a score of 546 for 3 hardly constituted a crisis, except for Australia and Eddie Paynter, who was a philosophic sort of chap possibly considered that it was the Australians who needed a little help for a change.

Paynter, born in Oswaldtwistle and Lancashire to the marrow, was as philosophical about his cricket as he was about life itself. He had all the qualities that Rudyard Kipling in his much quoted poem enumerated as the prerequisites for the complete man. He walked with crowds and kept his virtue, he talked with kings and kept the common touch, he treated alike the twin imposters triumph and disaster, and assuredly there was no man who filled better the unforgiving minute with sixty seconds worth of distance run.

When he was not batting and eager for runs, he was sprinting along the outfield to cut off a ball that had only a brief moment earlier seemed certain to reach the boundary, and quick as a whippet, he would gather it up and hurl it accurately into the wicket-keeper's gloves. He was there not only to save runs, but to get the batsman out if he possibly could, and he never allowed anyone to forget it.

For ten years he played with the Lancashire side in the 1930's; the sadness is that twelve more of his green years were lost to the game to which he gave so much. In his first-class career he scored 45 centuries, 36 for Lancashire, 4 for England, 3 for M.C.C touring sides and 2 in Festival games. His performances in the

1938 Test series against Australia were followed in the 1938-9 tour of South Africa by hundreds in each innings of the Johannesburg Test and 243 in the third Test at Durban.

Paynter's score of 216 not out in the Nottingham Test of 1938 established a new record as the highest score made by an England batsman against Australia. It was broken twice in the same series – by Hammond at Lord's and by Hutton at the Oval, and it has been exceeded since. One of his records, however, still stands. No other England batsman has made double centuries against both Australia and South Africa.

Memories of Eddie Paynter are green at Old Trafford, and long will they remain so. His 36 hundreds for Lancashire between 1931 and 1939 included four double centuries and a treble.

The treble hundred was made against Sussex at Hove in 1937 after the Lancashire team had travelled overnight from Manchester to Brighton. With little sleep, and only breakfast to sustain him when he first went to the wicket, Paynter made 322 of a total of 640 for 8 in five hours. He and Washbrook put on 268 for the first wicket, and must have allowed their grateful colleagues time for a little more rest than they had been able to get in their southward journey. In a second double century stand, he put on 271 for the third wicket with Oldfield in 2¼ hours.

Against Hampshire at Southampton a year later, he scored 291, and again with Oldfield he shared in a partnership of 306 for the third wicket. This is still a Lancashire third-wicket record.

'Roses' matches usually brought forth the best of Eddie Paynter. Not for him the negative doctrine of no fours before lunch on the first day. A bad ball was a bad ball to Paynter whether it was bowled at Headingley or Old Trafford or Weston-super-Mare, and a bad ball he would hit at whatever stage of the game it was sent down. In this approach to the game, Paynter had consciously adopted the philosophy of his great mentor, J.T. Tyldesley who had taught him never to be content with negative tactics or to allow the bowler to dictate terms. He believed that if the bowler had the advantage of a favourable wicket or weather conditions, then it behoved the batsman all the more to be aggressive and to show the bowler who was master. It was an admirable philosophy, and if it did not always succeed, there is evidence enough in the records that many of Paynter's finest and most belligerent innings were played on difficult wickets. The Yorkshire match at Bradford at Whitsuntide in 1932 will assuredly be associated with the name of Eddie Paynter so long as these games are played. On a bad wicket, with Verity bowling at his artful best, and partners leaving him in quick succession, he took upon himself the taming of the chief tormentor by cracking him aggressively round the field, punching him for four sixes and Leyland for another, just to show his impartiality. He scored his hundred out of 149, and went on to make 152 of Lancashire's 263. Verity had him at last, stumped in chasing a widish ball that most likely he had been seeing in terms of yet another six. It was a gloriously defiant, thrillingly pugnacious knock, and on that terrible wicket it put Lancashire in a position from which they won by an innings. That innings was typical of Paynter's outlook and of J.T. Tyldesley's. Some of the curiosities of Paynter's batting technique, however, must have amused and probably horrified Johnny who was much more inclined to the orthodox. Eddie Paynter was a small man, but he never considered his lack of inches a disadvantage. Some of his strokes brought shudders from the purists, often he seemed to get his bat and his pads in a fearful tangle, and he has even been known to go into a shot with both feet off the ground.

Certainly his technique could not be unreservedly recommended to a young batsman, though in Paynter's great heart, wonderful courage and aggressive approach the young player could have no finer model.

The strength and effectiveness of his batting lay ultimately in his keen eye and nimble footwork. His eye enabled him to decide early what stroke he would play, and he used his feet with the speed and agility of a ballet dancer to get to the pitch of the ball. Though he could play a waiting game if need be and the interests of his side demanded it, defensive cricket was as foreign to his nature as thrift would have been to Diamond Jim Brady.

He could play every stroke in the book as well as a good many that aren't in any book, though surprisingly those shots that I always thought of as his 'curiosities' were usually fashioned with the minimum risk. He had the facility of the great batsman for turning any ball's length into the length he wanted to make it, and for so small a man he charged his strokes with tremendous power. Towards the end of a long innings, even on the warmest

K

of days, he could be punching the ball as forcefully as when he had first gone in to bat.

His driving was firm and penetrating, his hooking fierce and uncompromising and he had a characteristic stroke, played wide of gully, something between a cut and a slash which sent the ball scorching to the boundary and brought him many runs.

After the war Eddie Paynter was seen no more as a player on the county cricket fields of England, and lovers of good cricket, not only in Lancashire, but all over the country and in the lands overseas where the game is played were well aware that a vital, expressive and colourful character had gone from it.

He played for some years in Bradford League cricket when his days in the first-class game were finished. Maybe his feet were not so nimble as when they brought him from his bed in that Brisbane hospital to play a Test-saving innings that set England on a winning way. Maybe his eye was not so keen as when he tore an Australian attack to shreds at Lord's and Trent Bridge and bludgeoned the South African bowlers into submission at Johannesburg and Durban.

Maybe his arm was not so strong as when he tamed Hedley Verity on that treacherous wicket at Bradford and showed Lancashire cricketers what a Lancashire batsman could do to a Yorkshire bowler, even of Verity's class and repute, if he had the courage, resolution and plain, honest guts.

No one relished a crisis or a fight more and if I were asked to choose a Lancashire team from all the ages to play the Rest of the World the name of Eddie Paynter would be in it.

He brought pleasure to many a Saturday afternoon of my youth, and we in Lancashire have our hopes that one day, like the legendary Arthur, a batsman endowed with all his splendid virtues will come again.

XX

Cyril Washbrook

Cyril Washbrook opened Lancashire's innings with Eddie Paynter in the years before the second World War, and he must in their partnership have absorbed some of the craft, discipline and technical knowledge of his older colleague. They certainly achieved a remarkable understanding and their running between the wickets was a joy to see. Both were fleet of foot, and to watch them scampering their runs rather than flickering to and fro as Francis Thompson's heroes did in earlier days, was an experience never to be forgotten.

A cool, unruffled temperament Cyril Washbrook had possessed from his youth and no other person could have given him that. Eddie Paynter, however was an early model, for Washbrook was born and spent his earlier years at Barrow near Blackburn where Paynter at one time played for the local club side as an amateur. Every Saturday the young Washbrook would watch the club's games in the Ribblesdale League, studying and admiring the speed of Paynter's fielding at cover. He would have noticed particularly that Paynter was a little man, and as Washbrook was not inclined to tallness himself, consciously or unconsciously he must have assimilated a good deal of Paynter's technique and aggressive approach to the game.

At school, both at Barrow and at Bridgnorth in Shropshire where the family moved, Washbrook was considered something of a cricketing prodigy. He spent much of his spare time during the summer at the nets of the local clubs, and at Bridgnorth Grammar School it was not long before he was playing for the school first XI and also for the second XI of the local club. From the club second team he soon progressed to the first XI, and in his first summer at Bridgnorth he scored well over a thousand runs, playing for both teams. Scouts from Lancashire, Warwickshire and Worcestershire county clubs became interested in his performances. Lancashire and Warwickshire offered him games with their minor county sides, and ultimately at the age of sixteen he was offered terms to join the respective ground staffs. Now there came family deliberations. His father wanted him to stay on at school with a view to University entrance, but he had failed one of his School Certificate examinations, and rather than remain at his studies to retake the examination, he pleaded with his father to allow him to become a cricketer. Finally the wise parent agreed to give the boy his chance, with the provision that if there seemed little prospect of his gaining a place in the county side after one season, he would abandon the idea of a cricketing career and seek more secure employment.

Warwickshire's were the more attractive terms as the Edgbaston authorities offered to assist with his fees if there were any likelihood of his taking a University degree and provided for winter pay which Lancashire's did not. He decided however to join Lancashire as the county of his birth, and also, one suspects, because his hero Eddie Paynter now wore the cap with the red rose.

When he reported to Old Trafford he came under the shrewd eye of Harry Makepeace and Washbrook himself has recorded in his book of autobiography the debt he owed Makepeace for the wise counsel the old cricketer gave him and the care he took to ensure that the youngster had adequate practice at the nets against all types of bowling. His first minor counties game as a member of the ground staff was in a testing 'rosebuds' match with Yorkshire second XI at Bradford in 1933. He distinguished himself by scoring an unbeaten double century. Playing in the same game, though not so successfully, was a young Yorkshireman, some eighteen months younger named Leonard Hutton. More that a decade and a world war later the two men were to open the England innings together.

Washbrook's first appearance for the county side was against Sussex at Old Trafford. He batted at No. 5 in the first innings and was out l.b.w. for 7. In the second, with a draw inevitable, he was sent in first and scored 40, hooking and cutting the renowned Maurice Tate with an assurance almost amounting to impudence. His next first-class game was against Surrey, also at Old Trafford. Alf Gover was the fastest bowler he had faced to that time, redoubtable, persevering and accurate. In a remarkable innings, not conspicuously noted for its orthodoxy, the young man scored 152 and went to his first county century with four successive boundaries, all from trenchant hooks. A century against Surrey, made in such confident fashion was a wonderful start for a young cricketer and it set the pavilion greybeards to comparisons with J.T. Tyldesley of immortal memory. But it was not to be a progress of continuous success. In his next three games, batting lower down the order, his aggregate was only 15. He returned to form, however against the West Indies tourists at Aigburth, scoring 95 himself and taking part with Len Hopwood in a stand of 200. He did not play in the 'roses' match at Headingley, but at the ground he met George Hirst, then the Yorkshire coach who was not averse to giving advice to a young Lancastrian, even though the white rose might suffer for it at some time or another. Hirst urged him never to be satisfied, even though he might be playing well. It was a counsel of perfection which Washbrook never forgot and which conditioned his cricketing outlook and attitude throughout his long career.

The 1935 season was, for Washbrook, the summer of decision. He must succeed in keeping his place in the county side, or, in accordance with the arrangement he had made with his father, turn his attentions to another means of earning a living. Happily for him, and for Lancashire and England cricket, his natural grit and talent surmounted all hazards. In a game at Oxford against the University he scored 228 out of 431. Against Worcestershire, facing Perks at his quickest and batting first on a lively wicket, he carried his bat through both Lancashire innings and was awarded his county cap. That season he scored over 1700 runs at an average of something over 45.

Lancashire did not have a good season in 1936, and though Washbrook scored more than a thousand runs, including centuries against the Indian tourists and Somerset, he could hardly be said to have fulfilled the promise of the previous year. The wet wickets of that summer were probably as much to blame as anything else, but Washbrook was the first to realize that, as a Lancashire cricketer and subject to damp pitches more than the players of other counties, he must learn at all costs to adapt his technique to them.

He did not start any more propitiously in 1937, and after a string of indifferent scores he was put back into the second team to give him an opportunity to regain his confidence. Harry Makepeace was patient with the young man as only that experienced old cricketer could be and the combination of

Makepeace's wisdom and Washbrook's determination could not fail to succeed. At last he scored a hundred in a minor counties game and back he went into the county side. In his first game on his return he scored 72 against Leicestershire and followed that up with 121 not out at Northampton. During his next ten innings he made a hundred against Surrey at Old Trafford and two against Sussex at Aigburth and Hove. In six matches he scored 670 runs and his run of success gained him a late place in the Oval Test match against New Zealand, when Eddie Paynter, who had originally been picked to play, was obliged to withdraw through injury. George Duckworth, another wise Lancastrian advised him to look to his fielding as well as to his batting, and Washbrook followed his counsel to such effect that in a match spoiled by rain his fielding was remembered. The Lancashire side of this period was not particularly strong in fielding, but in Paynter and Washbrook they had two masters of the craft. The keenness and enthusiasm of these two did much to raise the team's out-cricket. Above all the understanding they achieved as opening batsmen, their quickness between the wickets and their shrewd judgement of the short run were prime factors in the success of their association which was unfortunately cut short by the outbreak of war in 1939.

In the two seasons immediately preceeding the war Washbrook consolidated his place in the Lancashire team. He hit five centuries in 1938, including an unbeaten double century against Gloucestershire at Bristol, but he was not invited to play in a representative game and in the Test series with Australia it was his Lancashire partner Paynter and his future England partner Hutton who held the stage. In 1939 he scored well over 1600 runs at an average approaching 40, but there was no century among them. This record argued well for his consistency, but it is hundreds that catch the eyes of selectors and he was not picked for Tests against the West Indies.

During war service with the R.A.F. Washbrook played all the cricket he could and in 1945 he took part in the so-called 'Victory Tests' which were staged in England at the end of hostilities. In three of these games he opened the innings with Hutton. Twice they scored over 50 together, a significant augury of things to come.

County cricket started in earnest again in 1946, and in that season Washbrook scored 2400 runs in all matches at an average of over 68. These runs included nine hundreds. He was picked for England in the Tests against India and at Old Trafford, on a difficult wicket he and Hutton showed something of their true mettle in a stand of 81. *Wisden* chose him as one of its 'Five Cricketers of the Year', praising him as 'a handsome stroke player' and 'a cover-point worthy to be mentioned in the same breath as Hobbs.'

He was chosen to tour Australia and New Zealand with Hammond's side in the winter of 1946/47, a tour undertaken at the urgent request of the Australian cricket and political authorities who were anxious that Test cricket should be resumed as soon as possible. It was still too early after the long war to send out a fully representative, well-balanced England side. The Australians started with a distinct advantage for they already had the nucleus of a Test team in the Australian Forces side which had played together during the war years and in the 'Victory Tests'. In the event England lost the series and failed to win a single Test.

Hutton and Washbrook opened the England innings in all five matches. This series marked the beginning of their association as England's first-wicket pair and as protagonists of the formidable Australian speed attack of Lindwall and Miller at their fiercest. In the massacre at Brisbane, when England had so much the worse of the wicket, their contributions, both individually and in partnership were not impressive. Australia won again at Sydney, Washbrook scoring 41 in England's second innings, though he was overshadowed by Hutton, whose 37 was considered by those that saw it to be one of the finest innings of the series by an England batsman. In the third Test at Melbourne Washbrook achieved a personal triumph, scoring 62 out of 179 in England's first innings and 112, his first Test Century in the second. Both innings were predominantly defensive, though he hit a six and eight fours in his hundred. His batting in this game assuredly went a long way to earning England an honourable draw.

At Adelaide the match was again drawn, and Washbrook and Hutton gave their finest performance as openers with two century partnerships. Their stands realized 137 and 100 exactly. Washbrook missed his own hundred by only half a dozen runs in the first innings and he hit 39 in the second. In the last Test which England lost by five wickets Washbrook was summarily dismissed in Lindwall's first over. In the second innings he scored 24 and only Denis Compton made more. In State and other matches

outside the Tests Washbrook had a successful tour, though the
Australian crowds were rarely granted the pleasure of seeing him
in full-flow in an innings of uninhibited stroke-play. His work in
the field, however earned him plenty of praise and it soon became
a cricket axiom that to attempt to steal a run while the ball was
anywhere within Washbrook's reach was tantamount to batting
suicide.

Back in England in 1947, in a summer of glorious sunshine and
wonderful batting wickets, Washbrook was soon among the
runs. In that season he scored over 2,600, average 68. His eleven
hundreds included unbeaten double centuries against Sussex and
Surrey at Old Trafford. His innings in the Surrey match saved
the game for Lancashire who had gone in to bat a second time,
287 runs behind. In 6½ hours of vigilance, occasionally enlivened by aggression he scored 251 not out, denying Surrey the
victory they thought had been theirs. Washbrook seems to have
enjoyed the Sussex bowling more than most, for following his
unbeaten double century at Old Trafford earlier in the season, he
hit hundreds in both innings of the return game at Eastbourne,
176 and 121 not out, giving him an aggregate of 501 runs for only
once out.

Over the next seasons runs flowed prolifically from Washbrook's bat, and his qualities as an opener, with Hutton for his
country or with Place for his county, were acknowledged and
admired wherever cricket was played. With Place he participated
in many a fruitful first-wicket partnership for Lancashire and the
firm foundation which they gave to an innings in the years of
their association was envied by most other county sides, not so
fortunately blessed. In the games with Sussex, mentioned earlier,
they took part in opening stands of 350 at Old Trafford and 233 at
Eastbourne (both unbroken). Their understanding and judgement of a run were as marked in their association for Lancashire
as were those of Washbrook and Hutton for England.

Washbrook played in four of the five Tests against Australia in
1948, missing the match at the Oval through injury. The
Australian attack was again spearheaded by Lindwall and Miller
and was as strong and varied as any captain of a touring side ever
had at his command. Washbrook played the fast bowling
confidently and courageously, though he sometimes had fierce
bruises to show for it. He averaged over 50 and scored more runs
than any other England batsman except Compton. At Old

Trafford he hit 85 not out in England's second innings and looked well set for a century when a declaration was made in an abortive attempt to win the match. At Headingley he scored 143 in the first innings and 65 in the second and he shared with Hutton in a century opening stand in each innings, a performance which established a new world record, for the feat had never before been accomplished twice by the same batsmen. Sadly this fine batting was of no avail, for Australia won the match, after being set to score 404 to win in the last innings.

Washbrook toured South Africa with the M.C.C. side in 1948/49, averaged 60 for the tour and played a lively and significant part in the Tests. In the second Test at Johannesburg he and Hutton set up a new record for an opening partnership in Test matches. Their stand of 359, made in exhausting conditions on a bakingly hot day, 6,000 feet above sea level, surpassed by 36 runs the previous record set up by Hobbs and Sutcliffe in 1912. Washbrook was out only five runs short of a double century. He had indulged himself generously in his favourite square-cuts and hooks, but as he subsequently revealed, by that time he was so tired that he could scarcely swing his bat at all. The stand was the highest made by Washbrook and Hutton together and it lasted ten minutes short of five hours. The fourth Test of the series was played on the same ground, and in this Washbrook failed by only three runs to make another hundred. He had hooked the previous ball for six, but in attempting to repeat the stroke he was caught.

Washbrook was frequently accused of rashness for playing the hook shot, particularly in Test Matches and a fieldsman was usually stationed for a catch when he was taking strike. He was always aware that he was taking a calculated risk, but he would argue that the stroke brought him many runs in the course of a season.

He played in two of the four Tests against the strong West Indies team in 1950 and only injury kept him out of the other two, for he was one of the more successful batsmen in a series in which those two formidable spinners Ramadhin and Valentine caused such bewilderment and created such havoc. In the second Test at Lord's, with wickets tumbling about him, his 114 in 5½ hours, though hardly a characteristic Washbrook innings, was a splendid gesture of brave defiance. At Trent Bridge Worrell and Weekes had so savaged the England bowling that West Indies were far ahead on the first innings. Washbrook and Simpson

(Hutton was absent injured) raised hopes of England's saving the game with a partnership of 212 for the first wicket. Washbrook's share was 102, but the effort was in vain, for the later batting collapsed and West Indies won comfortably.

Washbrook's tour of Australia in the winter of 1950/51 with F. R. Brown's side was not, for him, so successful as his previous tour and he was not picked for the home Tests against South Africa in 1951 or against India in 1952. He was still out of favour for the next two series with Australia in England in 1953 and in Australia in 1954/5. So the great partnership was dissolved. Never again did Hutton and Washbrook open an England innings together. Whilst it lasted it was a notable association, and like Shakespeare's Moor they did the State some service. The picture of the two of them, walking through the pavilion gate onto the field lingers pleasantly in the memory. Both walked easily, relaxed but purposeful, Washbrook the shorter but thicker set, with strong forearms, cap at a jaunty angle, Hutton, slighter in build, not so square at the shoulder, cap soberly correct, forearms scarcely suggesting the strength of his partner, yet every movement indicative of the superb athlete he was.

They played as if by instinct as natural partners, adjusting their tactics to the state of the wicket, the climatic conditions, the strength of the attack and the field placings or the needs of their side as dictated by the state of the game. The record of their opening partnerships is illuminating. On eight occasions they shared century stands for England, five times against Australia, twice against South Africa and once against New Zealand. They are still the holders of the record first-wicket stand for England and in the 1946/47 series in Australia they made three century opening stands in consecutive innings. On twenty occasions they opened innings in Test matches with stands of 50 or more. Fifty times they opened together for England and here again the record is impressive. Against Australia they scored in partnership 1042 runs at an average of 49·61, against South Africa 1371 runs at 80.64, against West Indies 90 at 45, against India 152 at 38 and against New Zealand 177 at 44·25. The aggregate figures for all Tests are 2832 runs at an average of 59.

Washbrook was recalled to Test Cricket in 1956 under quite remarkable circumstances. He was then 42 years of age, an elder statesman of cricket, though he was still playing for Lancashire and had been appointed to the Test Selection Committee at the beginning of the season. England were holding the 'Ashes', retained in Australia in 1954/55, but after two Tests Australia were one up in the series. For the third Test at Headingley it was essential that the batting be strengthened, for if Australia were to win again, England could virtually write off the series. Though Washbrook had played only a handful of innings that season for Lancashire, his name was suggested at the Selection Committee meeting, and he left the room whilst the suggestion was discussed by his colleagues. Peter May, the captain was initially opposed to Washbrook's selection, probably on the grounds of his age and the possibility of lessened mobility in the field, but the majority were in favour of his inclusion. It was well for England's chances of keeping the 'Ashes' that they were, and later May generously admitted it.

On the morning of the match England won the toss and batted. Lindwall and Archer were formidably fast and accurate, but it was Archer, bowling with a breeze that blew diagonally across the wicket, who wreaked early havoc. He made the ball swing sharply and late and he had Cowdrey, Oakman and Richardson back in the pavilion for 17 runs at a cost of only three to himself. When Washbrook came in at the fall of the third wicket to join his captain it was to the sort of situation he relished. There was no trace of apprehension or nervousness in his face or bearing and his cap, as always was cocked jauntily over his left eye. The Yorkshire crowd cheered him as loudly as if it bore the crest of the white rose. They knew him well as a stern and honoured opponent in many a 'roses' argument.

Washbrook survived an appeal for l.b.w. when he had scored only 3, but with that episode behind him he and May set to work to redeem England's fortunes. The early fire of Archer and Lindwall was extinguished, and through the rest of the day the two batsmen withstood the Australian attack. Their batting was by no means defensive in conception despite the precarious situation in which they had come together. Each ball was treated strictly on its merits, and punishment was handed out to any deserving it. Throughout the afternoon and early evening they treated the Headingley crowd to a delectable display of the batsman's art. May drove gracefully, cracking the ball powerfully through the field, Washbrook's square and late cutting and inevitably his hooking put the bowling ruthlessly to the sword. After tea the new ball was taken and all the fire and fury of the opening attack in the morning was called back into being. The gloss had been taken from the new ball, the stand had passed 150 and May had gone to his century, when just as it was seeming that the two would be there to continue next morning, May was out shortly before close of play.

There can have been nobody on the ground the following morning, apart from those perverse oddities who never like to see virtue triumphant, who did not wish for Washbrook the full reward of a hundred for his splendid cricket of the day before. He had taken his score to 98 when the field was brought in closer to prevent his taking a run from the last ball of an over by Benaud. That last ball was short, but not short enough to play his favourite hook shot for which Washbrook had positioned himself. It kept low and clipped him on the pad. Benaud's appeal was automatic and Washbrook saw the umpire's finger raised against him.

For a long moment the crowd seemed stunned to silence, then as Washbrook walked from the wicket, head high, cap still at its jaunty angle, the enormity of what had happened seeped through. A hundred is a hundred in the record books, ninety eight just another score. But that 98 of Washbrook's at Heading-ley against Australia will never be reckoned just another score in the ordinary sense. Without him who could have stood so long in the breach with May? Their fourth wicket stand not only produced precious runs, it also bought valuable time and went a long way towards winning the game for England. Though he was picked for the fourth and fifth Tests Washbrook did not reproduce his Headingley form. Albeit he will be remembered in that 1956 series for his glittering day when the odds were stacked against his country and he did not fail the challenge.

Washbrook's career spanned nearly twenty years, though the war sadly took away from it what could have been the years of greatest achievement. He played in 37 Test matches and scored 2569 runs at an average of nearly 43, but there is little doubt that had he been able to play in Tests between 1940 when he was 26 and 1945 when he was 31, the years in a batsman of ripening experience and increasing maturity, not only his aggregate but also his average would have been markedly higher. For Lancashire, Washbrook played in just 500 matches and scored nearly 28,000 runs at an average of over 42. Only the Tyldesley brothers had higher aggregates and Washbrook's average is second only to Ernest's in the Lancashire records. He scored 76 centuries during his career, less than either of the Tyldesleys, but more that any other Lancashire batsman.

In 1954 he became Lancashire's first professional captain when he succeeded Nigel Howard, and he captained the county side for six seasons until his retirement from active cricket in 1959. He may not be rated one of the greatest or more successful Lancashire captains, for it can be argued that his captaincy was inclined too much to rigidity. Certainly he appeared to lack the imagination essential to a good captain, and he often seemed disinclined to take a calculated risk which a successful leader should always be prepared to essay. It is said that he was too stern a disciplinarian. Discipline, however, is essential to a team and no side can expect to go far without it. Assuredly Washbrook was always a perfectionist; he set a high standard for himself and when he became captain of Lancashire it could have come as no surprise that he would expect a similar standard of those who played under him.

The acid test of a good leader in any sphere of activity is that he should be capable of combining the maintenance of discipline with a broad humanity, recognizing that all men are not endowed with the same talents and sensitivities, and exercising at all times a sympathetic understanding of human failings and frailties. If Washbrook failed to measure up to that ultimate yardstick, and showed a certain intolerance to those whom he considered fell below his own standards, it should be remembered how difficult it is for a man who is a perfectionist himself to accept anything less in others. Though Lancashire never won the County Championship during Washbrook's captaincy, they had a very useful side, capable of mature and attractive cricket.

In the final estimate of Washbrook's batting it will probably be reckoned that he fell somewhere short of greatness. Certainly he was not blessed with the genius of his great contemporaries, Hammond, Hutton and Compton, but on his day and with his full range of strokes he would not have suffered by comparison with any of them. First and foremost he was a stroke-player. Defensive cricket irked him, though his defensive technique was as complete and all-embracing as one might expect of a pupil of Harry Makepeace. He thoroughly disliked to have bowlers dictating the course of a game, and there was no more exciting prospect in Washbrook's years as a Lancashire opener than to watch him start an innings, front foot cocked arrogantly at the bowler or champing impatiently at the opposite end as non-striker.

His defensive batting, though set in a minor key, was never dull to watch. The diligent care with which he treated every ball and the fascination of watching him select the right stroke or even the degree of strokelessness for each one, made even the quietest Washbrook innings an occasion to remember. But to see him in full spate, spraying the field with all his lovely strokes as he ripped into attack was an experience to savour as one of cricket's supreme pleasures. There are those who contend that he never fulfilled the promise of his early years, that he should have scored more runs in Test and county cricket. Had it not been for the lost war years he would have scored many more runs in both spheres, and he would almost certainly have surpassed Ernest Tyldesley's record aggregate for Lancashire.

If the critics imply that he achieved a considerable competence rather than the greatness which might have been his, they are on safer ground. His record does not match, for example, the wonderful consistency of Hutton, and it is a fact that he got out, when seemingly well set, more frequently than some of his great contemporaries. The famous hook, often a lucrative source of runs, too often the cause of his dismissal, was one of the chinks in his armour. Another was a curious immobility of the feet, which one would have thought in a batsman with Washbrook's desire for perfection might have been eradicated earlier, a defect in his technique or a quirk of nature, call it what you will, which often, and particularly in his later years, had him leg-before-wicket.

In the field, at cover, he was one of the finest ever, worthy to rank with Hobbs or Bradman, or with Lancashire's own Vernon Royle, probably the finest of them all. But whatever his rating in English cricket there are few who would deny that Washbrook was one of the 'characters' of the game in the years he played it. The angle at which he wore his cap, the forward thrust of his chest and the seemingly slight swagger in his walk might have suggested arrogance, but he was never an arrogant man, just a supremely confident one.

For one season after his retirement from active cricket he undertook an experimental appointment as team manager of the county side. It was years before the sort of appointment became more common, but the innovation was not a success and his appointment was not renewed after the first season of trial. His great services to Lancashire and England cricket, however, were by no means ended. He was later elected to the County Committee where it is certain he brought ripe experience and sage counsel to its deliberations. He became a Test selector and served for several seasons on the Selection Committee.

Since Cyril Washbrook first came to Old Trafford as a raw youngster with the light of ambition in his eye he has become such an important part of the Lancashire cricket scene that it would be difficult indeed to imagine the place without him. As player, captain, administrator and Test selector he has lived a full cricketing life and has given much enjoyment in living it wherever the game is played.

XXI

Dick Pollard and Roy Tattersall

Dick Pollard, like Dick Tyldesley a man of Westhoughton, first played for Lancashire County in 1933 and between then and his retirement from first class cricket in 1950 he took 1015 wickets (1119 in all matches) at 22 runs apiece.

Like Eddie Paynter, Cyril Washbrook and many another good cricketer the war took a hefty slice from his first-class career; instead of taking wickets for Lancashire he was bowling out service sides. It is of some moment to reflect that, had it not been for those missing seasons Pollard could have challenged or even surpassed the wonderful records of Brian Statham and Johnny Briggs as wicket-takers for his county.

In the years immediately preceding and following the war the sight of this burly, great hearted fast-medium bowler, toiling uncomplainingly through the heat and burden of the day epitomized the spirit and traditions of Lancashire cricket. There was no more appropriate symbol of good honest industry than Dick Pollard, with a full head of steam, hurling down his thunderbolts over after over. His russet hair was cropped close to his skull and his countenance glowed pinkly in the sun.

It is said that a pace bowler isn't worth his salt if he hasn't a fiery temper to give his bowling that little bit extra 'edge', but I fancy the sentiment originated across the Pennines, where Yorkshire have had, in the course of their history, a not inconsiderable number of bowlers who have fulfilled that requirement. Certainly I have, in my time, known none in Lancashire, and I don't think that Ted McDonald or Dick Pollard or Brian Statham can be so lightly dismissed because of a lack of fire and brimstone in their make-up.

Not for any of them the curious scowl down the wicket or at the umpire, the hands raised to high Heaven in despairing disbelief at the rank injustice of a bowler's lot. They accepted the slings and arrows of outrageous fortune, the streaky shots off the edge and the occasional lapses in the slips with the philosophical calm of the long-suffering. Pollard's nickname of th' owd chain horse was not bestowed lightly. 'Owd chain horses are not noted for complaining. Nor was he.

He took 100 wickets in a season for the first time in 1936, and repeated the achievement every summer until his retirement from first-class cricket, with the single exception of the 1946 season, the first after the end of the war, when he was still serving with the forces and missed a number of matches.

His best season was in 1947 when he took 137 wickets for Lancashire after touring Australia with the M.C.C. side the previous winter. He performed the 'hat-trick' twice – against Glamorgan at Preston in 1939 and against Warwickshire at Blackpool in 1947. Three times in his career he took eight wickets in an innings and in the Middlesex game at Old Trafford in 1946 his match record was 14 for 216 runs.

Test recognition came late to Pollard, but here again the war was largely to blame. His first game for England was in the second Test against India at Old Trafford in 1946. In India's first innings he and Alec Bedser shared nine of the wickets, Pollard 5 for 24, Bedser 4 for 41. When India batted a second time Bedser withered all before his blast and took 7 wickets for 52 runs. Pollard's contribution (2 for 63) looks less spectacular on paper, but his two victims were the openers, Merchant and Mustaq Ali who had participated in a century stand in the first innings. Pollard had Merchant caught for a 'duck' and clean bowled Mustaq for 1.

He did not play in the last Test at the Oval, and though he toured Australia and New Zealand with Hammond's side in the winter of 1946/47, he was not chosen for any of the Tests in Australia, though he played in the one Test in New Zealand at the end of the tour. No less an authority than Sir Donald Bradman found Pollard's omission from the Australian Tests rather strange.

Opinions expressed by Australians about English cricketers have often been regarded with a certain amount of suspicion. They have been accused of playing or persuading an indifferent bowler into an England Test side by showing exaggerated respect for him in State or County matches, only to put him remorselessly to the sword when this apparent respect induced the ingenuous selectors to play him in a Test. To Bradman's view of the non-selection of Pollard for that particular Test series an ulterior motive certainly cannot be ascribed, for it was expressed after both he and Pollard had retired from active cricket.

Though Pollard had such a good season in 1947, he was not picked for any of the Tests against South Africa that summer, and he had to wait until the following year when the Australians were touring England for his next call to the colours. Then possibly to test the efficacy of the old maxim about picking horses for courses, the' owd chain horse was picked for the third Test at Old Trafford. In this game he took the wickets of Bradman, Miller and Loxton in 32 overs at a cost of 53 runs in Australia's first innings, a not insignificant performance

In the next Test at Headingley Pollard took Bradman's wicket again in Australia's first innings and also that of Hassett. His match figures in a game in which Australia scored 862 runs and no English bowler distinguished himself were 2 wickets for 159 runs, and although other bowlers who had been well drubbed at Headingley were picked again for England, Pollard was not.

His Test record for two games against Australia, one against India and one against New Zealand was 15 wickets at 25 runs apiece in 183 overs. There was a greater potential of service to his country in Dick Pollard than those figures suggest. The pity was that it was not realized – either by him or by the selectors.

It was for Lancashire that he will always be remembered as one of the greatest triers who ever played for the county. I fancy that as he took his cricket bag from Old Trafford for the last time, the knowledge that he was a member of the very select band of bowlers who have taken over a thousand wickets for Lancashire was sufficient reward for his years of honest toil.

Roy Tattersall, another fine bowler from the Bolton area who took more than a thousand wickets for the county (1168 at 17 runs each) came comparatively late to first-class cricket. He was 26 when he played in his first game for Lancashire in 1948, and it was not until 1950 that he was awarded his county cap, but his advance was rapid and in that summer of 1950 his remarkable record in all matches read:-

Overs	Maidens	Runs	Wkts	Average
1404.4	502	2623	193	13.59

He took, in that season, more wickets with his off-breaks and cutters than any other bowler in first-class cricket and his record bettered those of Ramadhin and Valentine, the West Indian magicians who were creating such alarm and despondency among English batsmen. It is an unjust world as W.S. Gilbert's Mikado so rightly observed, and virtue is so often triumphant only in theatrical performances. It should have come as no surprise, therefore, though numerous loyal Lancastrians were rightly incensed that Tattersall's virtues as an off-spinner, and what is more, an off-spinner in commanding form, went unrecognized and he was not picked to play in any of the Test matches that summer. Nor was he originally chosen as a member of the M.C.C. side to tour Australia during the winter. As the tour progressed, however, the team was plagued by injuries, and the selectors remembered Tattersall's record. With his county colleague Brian Statham, he was flown out from a chill English winter to strengthen M.C.C's stricken forces.

He had little opportunity to become acclimatized to Australian conditions before he was thrust into the crucible at Adelaide in the fourth Test. In these circumstances he did not succeed in reproducing his form of the summer. He claimed the wickets of Morris, a double centurion, Burke and Tallon in Australia's first innings for 95 runs. In the second innings he was not so successful, and Archer's wicket cost him over a hundred.

Perhaps the long look he was obliged to take at the methods of the Australian batsmen taught him something of batting technique, for it was with his batting in the last Test at Melbourne that he made some impact on the series.

Possibly Tattersall did not need to learn anything from the Australians. He used the method that he had always used when batting at No. 11 for Lancashire and would continue to use throughout his cricketing career, the method that was the cause of much hilarity among the members at Old Trafford. and which many likened to the contortions of a cricketing camel.

Tattersall had no false illusions about his style. He would clamp his back foot firmly inside the crease and dart forward with his bat towards the pitch of the ball, frequently more in fervent hope than from mature judgement.

The 'method' worked well enough at Melbourne, as it had worked in similar tight situations at Old Trafford and on other English cricket fields. When Tattersall came to the wicket England were 246 for 9, only 29 runs ahead of the Australian first innings total. Nothing much was expected of Tattersall as he walked out to join Simpson who had been in since the fall of the first wicket, and I imagine the Australians were already thinking of the rest they reckoned they would shortly be enjoying after their day in the field.

Against all expectations, however, Tattersall stayed with Simpson whilst 74 almost incredible runs were added for the last wicket, runs which completely changed the course of the game.

Miller contrived to defeat the forward prod at last, and Tattersall's share of that momentous partnership was 10, but the value of his innings could not be measured in terms of runs alone. England's ultimate lead of 103 was enough to give them their first win over Australia since the Oval Test in 1938.

Tattersall continued to baffle the best batsmen with his subtly flighted off-breaks and cutters, bowled from his considerable height and with a brisk pace from the pitch. In the Lord's Test against South Africa in 1951, on a rain affected wicket, he took 7 wickets for 52 in South Africa's first innings, and followed up this fine performance with 5 for 49 in the second.

He toured India in the winter of 1951/52 with N.D. Howard's side and played in all five Tests, bowling as economically as anyone on the hard wickets, and at Kanpur, on the one wicket helpful to bowlers in that series, he and Malcolm Hilton, his Lancashire colleague, mopped up the Indian batting. Tattersall's share of the harvest was 8 for 125.

Between 1951 and 1954 he played in sixteen Tests, and took 58 wickets at 26 runs apiece, but the rise of Laker and the preference of the selectors for the Surrey off-spinner caused the setting of Tattersall's star, at least so far as Test cricket was concerned.

For Lancashire he continued on his subtly consistent way, taking his hundred wickets a season. Six times he took eight or more wickets in an innings and in the Notts game at Old Trafford in 1953 he had the remarkable match analysis of 14 wickets for 73 runs including the 'hat-trick'.

In 1956 at Headingley his off-spin completely baffled the Yorkshire batsmen, and he took 6 wickets for 47 runs in their first innings and 8 for 43 in the second. This match analysis had only been bettered in 'roses' cricket by the Yorkshire bowler Peate who had taken 14 Lancashire wickets for 80 runs at Old Trafford 76 years earlier.

In 1958 his powers began to wane. He appeared to lose

confidence and some of his control, and it seemed that either the old tricks were beginning to fail or batsmen were 'reading' him better. Two years later his first-class career was over.

Tattersall, a modest and cheerful man and always a good humoured one, ever ready for a laugh at his own expense, was a highly popular figure in his years at Old Trafford. Affectionately known in the pavilion and on the popular side alike as 'Tatt' he rendered yeoman service to his county's cause and he was much missed when he had gone.

XXII

Brian Statham

Brian Statham first played for Lancashire in 1950, and in the nineteen seasons and nine M.C.C. tours between then and his retirement in 1968 he took 2259 wickets in all matches at 16·35 runs each. For Lancashire he took 1816 at slightly over 15. No bowler has taken more wickets for the county.

The most pronounced attributes of Statham's bowling were accuracy and economy. His career average in first-class cricket is better than that of Trueman, Barnes, Tate, Larwood, Grimmett, O'Reilly, Lindwall, Miller, Bedser or Laker. Of all these great bowlers O'Reilly (average 16·6) comes closest to Statham in economy.

In his 70 Test matches at home and overseas Statham claimed 252 wickets at 24·87 runs each, 69 against both Australia and South Africa, 42 against West Indies, 25 against India, 27 against Pakistan and 20 against New Zealand.

Somewhat surprisingly he became a cricketer almost by accident. As a boy he was not particularly interested in cricket, and preferred to play soccer or tennis. He played some cricket at school, but his interest seems to have ended there. He did not follow the game in the newspapers, and he once said that he doubted very much if he could have named half the England side during his schooldays.

It was whilst he was serving with the R.A.F. that he first turned his attention seriously to cricket, and it seems that he became interested partly by the fact that there were fewer opportunities for tennis in the summer months and partly because by playing cricket he could escape the monotony of clerical duties at his unit.

The Secretary of the unit team, impressed by the young airman's bowling ability, wrote to the Lancashire authorities suggesting that they should give him a trial at Old Trafford. Even at that time Statham was not enthusiastic, but Old Trafford was near to his home and attending for a trial meant a precious

leave pass, so he decided to take up the offer.
The day appointed for the trial arrived, but so did the rain, and he did not bother to go to the ground. Statham thought no more of the matter until the following spring, but Lancashire did not forget the unit team Secretary's recommendation. He received an invitation from Harry Makepeace, asking him to report to Old Trafford.
The trial was satisfactory, for only a fortnight after his demobilization Statham joined the ground staff. In his early county games he impressed by his speed and accuracy and in that initial season in first-class cricket he finished with the highly promising figures:-

Overs	Maidens	Runs	Wkts	Average
300·5	82	613	37	16.56

It was in the Yorkshire match at Old Trafford in August that he first gave notice to the cricket world that a new and exciting fast bowling prospect had arrived.
In that first taste of 'roses' cricket the young Statham found himself bowling his opening over to the great Leonard Hutton. Twice in his first three balls, he fell flat on the ground as he ran up to bowl on the somewhat slippery surface. He did not take Hutton's wicket, but in that opening spell he claimed those of Lowson, Lester and Watson at a cost of only 13 runs. All three batsmen were dismissed without scoring, and Lowson and Lester were clean bowled. He added to these early 'scalps' those of Halliday and Coxon and finished with the highly satisfactory figures of 5 for 52 in his first brush with the Old Enemy.
This performance remained in Hutton's memory, and when the M.C.C. side in Australia the following winter was severely handicapped by injuries to leading bowlers, Statham was flown out with his Lancashire colleague Roy Tattersall to reinforce the weakened party. He found that apart from Hutton and his fellow Lancastrians, Washbrook and Berry, he knew no other members of the M.C.C. team.
Going as he did, straight from an English winter to the sunshine and heat of the Antipodes, he found it difficult to acclimatize himself, and he could not strike form soon enough to be considered as a Test candidate in the matches with Australia. He did, however, gain his first England cap in New Zealand, and

he took the first of his many Test wickets.

In the 1951 season in England, his first full season in county cricket, he took 97 wickets at 15 runs apiece, topping Lancashire's bowling averages. He was to remain at the top for the next fifteen seasons. He played in two of the Tests against South Africa that season. taking 4 wickets for 78 runs.

Tours of India and Pakistan and the West Indies followed in the winters of 1951/52 and 1953/54, and between them Statham took over a hundred wickets in each of the home seasons 1952 and 1953. On the West Indies tour he played in four of the Tests, and on the concrete hard pitches, he took 16 wickets at 28 runs each.

In the Tests of 1954/55 in Australia with Frank Tyson as his partner as the spearhead of the attack, England retained the 'Ashes' they had won in 1953. The Tyson-Statham combination proved to be the decisive factor in that remarkable series.

England had been heavily beaten in the first Test at Brisbane, and for the second at Sydney, Alec Bedser who had been the mainstay of England's attack since the end of the war, was left out of the side. Hutton, England's captain, wanted the fastest opening attack available and that meant Tyson and Statham.

Australia won the toss in that second Test, put England in to bat, and shot them out again for a beggarly 154. Tyson, bowling at tremendous pace, Statham, fast and naggingly accurate and Bailey, admirable in control confined Australia to a first innings lead of 74 when it had seemed that it would be considerably longer. May and Cowdrey set England well on their way to their second innings total of 296, and Australia were set to make 223 to win. At the end of the fourth day they had made 72 for 2 and the game was nicely balanced.

Hutton did not use Tyson and Statham straight away on the last morning, but held them back until it seemed that Australia were coasting to victory. They proceeded to take the last five remaining wickets to give England a surprising win. Tyson claimed the lion's share of ten wickets in the match; Statham took only three, and as so often happened in their partnership, bowled against the wind for long periods, but his wonderful accuracy was as essential to the success of the enterprise as Tyson's speed.

At Melbourne in the third Test, Statham's fine bowling (5 for 60) in Australia's first innings restricted their lead to 40 after England had again batted first. England scored 279 in their second knock, and Australia wanted 240 to win.

At the end of the fourth day Australia had whittled 79 runs from their target and had lost two wickets. Once again the game was finely balanced, but this time Hutton brought on his fast bowlers immediately on the last morning.

In 80 minutes sensational cricket Australia's last eight wickets fell for 36 runs. Tyson took 6 wickets for 16 runs in 6 overs and 3 balls, Statham, 2 for 19 in 6 overs. Again Statham's strict accuracy and control were the perfect complement to Tyson's sheer pace.

At Adelaide the teams once more were evenly balanced after the first innings; England's slight advantage was 18 runs. The pitch was wearing when Australia batted again, and Hutton took off Statham after he had bowled only a couple of overs, bringing on Appleyard, who took three good wickets at the end of the fourth day.

Next morning it was expected that Appleyard would continue, but Hutton again turned to Tyson and Statham. The tactics were triumphantly justified. In an hour and a half Statham took 3 wickets for 12 runs, Tyson 3 for 17 and Australia were all out for 111. England needed only 94 to win, and despite an aggressive spell of bowling by Miller, they finished victors by 5 wickets.

The last Test was ruined by rain and drawn. It had been a triumphant series for England, Hutton and above all for Tyson and Statham. Tyson took 28 wickets, Statham 18. Tyson's speed and Statham's straightness had been the vital decisive factors. Sadly Tyson was never the same magnificent bowler again. He went from the first-class game, settled of all places in Australia and left the legend of his speed behind him. Statham's wonderful accuracy was sustained season in and season out for another fourteen years.

In the 1955 series with South Africa the partnership which had served England so well in Australia operated again in the first Test at Trent Bridge. It made significant inroads into the South African first innings batting, and on a pitch affected by rain Tyson swept away the second innings as he had routed the Australians the previous winter.

At Lord's where Tyson could not play, it was Statham who demoralized the South Africans in their second innings to help England to a win that had not, at one time, seemed possible. After England had been put out for 133 by the South African pace

bowlers, Heine, Adcock and Goddard, South Africa went to a
first innings lead of 171. England fared much better in their
second innings, thanks to fine, spirited batting by May,
Graveney and Compton and left South Africa to make 183 to
win, on the face of it a not too difficult task.

In the last half hour's play on the Saturday Statham took the
important wickets of McGlew and Goddard, and the South
African innings was shorn of its top. Monday's play was
interrupted for two hours by bad light, a delay which punctuated
a magnificent spell of bowling by Statham. He bowled unchanged through the innings for 29 overs to take 7 wickets for 39
and England won the match by 71 runs. In the four Tests of that
series in which he played he took 17 wickets at 21 runs apiece.

So Statham's splendid career in county and Test cricket
continued through the years. He bowled consistently fast and
straight and very rarely did it happen that a batsman had no need
to play a ball which he had bowled. It was said that he bowled too
straight and too accurately, that the batsman could always be
sure of his line, and that if he had deviated occasionally he would
have taken more wickets. This was a criticism that did not worry
Statham overmuch. He would say humourously that if he
bowled outside the off stump he would need his fieldsmen on the
off-side, if he bowled outside the leg stump he would need them
on the leg-side, but if he bowled straight at the stumps he
required only a wicket keeper. Seriously, his philosophy was
simple. He bowled straight at the stumps: if the batsman missed
he hit them. It was as uncomplicated as that.

There is no doubt that his unfailing accuracy helped many
another bowler to wickets. Batsmen could not take liberties with
Statham. What liberties they could take they took at the other
end and many found themselves walking back to the pavilion
when they did so.

In addition to his remarkable accuracy Statham possessed, for
a fast bowler, an unusually equable temperament. The frustrations which are part and parcel of the bowler's lot did not upset
him or affect his performance. There are those who contend that
Statham would have been a better bowler for the extra 'devil' of a
volatile temper. Possibly he might have taken more wickets;
certainly he would have been no better bowler.

In his career he got through a tremendous amount of hard
work, yet he would perform his long stints of bowling with a

philosophic dedication and a zest for the game that he was never to lose. Often in Test matches he was asked to bowl up-slope or into the breeze, to give a bowler at the other end who might be supposed to have an extra yard of pace the benefit of the conditions. It is doubtful if any other fast bowler in the history of cricket can have sustained such consistent accuracy over so many years as Brian Statham. The prospect of a hard day's trundling never deterred or disheartened him.

Once one of his Lancashire colleagues complained bitterly at the loss of a toss which seemed to make it inevitable that Lancashire would spend a long time in the field on a wicket all in favour of the batsmen. Statham's riposte was swift and revealing; 'We'll just have to bowl a bloody sight harder,' he said.

Statham's action did not meet with the unreserved approval of the classicists but it was smooth and effortless, the run-up silent and menacing as he accelerated over the last few paces, the delivery achieved with the feet almost together, a final thrust of his double-jointed shoulder and a whip of the wrist. In accordance with the best manuals of instruction his arm invariably brushed his right ear. Throughout the action, from bowling mark to final delivery, there was a smooth, flowing rhythm, never the slightest suggestion of brute force.

Statham was not a great swinger of the ball in the air, but off the pitch he could move it to compare with the greatest in the annals of the game, and he had a break-back that whipped in to the right-hander like lightning. Many were the wickets he took with this formidable ball, and it frequently confounded the best.

Beautifully and athletically built, lean as a whippet to which he was often likened, he could bowl on for over after over if need be, without flagging or complaint and with the same unremitting accuracy. A man of wry humour, at the end of a long stint of bowling, he would discuss in the dressing room the trials and tribulations of the day with his two aching feet.

Inevitably it will be asked in years to come, by people who never saw either bowl, which was the better bowler, Brian Statham or Frederick Sewards Trueman? It is a question on which their contemporary batsmen were probably about equally divided in their opinions. There were those who preferred to be facing Statham as Trueman was the less predictable of the two, and the more likely to produce the unplayable ball. There were others who would rather have faced Trueman because it was so difficult to score runs from Statham. If my own view, admittedly Lancastrian is that Statham was, day in and day out, the better bowler, let me record at once that both were unquestionably great ones, and in Test Cricket, when they were bowling together, their cumulative impact was considerably more forceful than the sum of their individual abilities.

Statham played his last Test match in the 1965 series against South Africa, when he was recalled for one game at the age of 35. He had taken no part in Test cricket since 1963 when he had played in two matches against the touring West Indians, not with conspicuous success as his figures (3 wickets for 243 runs) testify. What the figures do not show is the number of chances that were put down from his bowling.

In that one Test in 1965 he took 7 wickets for 145 runs to prove that on the international cricket scene he was still a force to be reckoned with. Yet with a modesty typical of the man, it was he who revealed his limitations. He had reached the time of life when five-day Test cricket was becoming rather more than he could comfortably manage, and though he appeared to be bowling with all his old skill and accuracy, he found that he tired more easily than in his salad years. Or rather, as he would say with a wry smile, Brian Statham might be willing, but his poor old feet, which had borne the main burden of his cricketing career, were not.

He was a magnificent out-field, and as one might expect of a fast bowler, he had a powerful, accurate throw and an invariably safe pair of hands. As a batsman, he summed up his own limitations as two 'strokes' - the straight-batted block and the cross-batted slog. His batting was usually treated hilariously at Old Trafford, but truth to tell, it could be better than most people, including he himself rated it. He could unleash, if he were so minded, an almost impeccable cover-drive, though most of his runs came from good old-fashioned mows and heaves. The occasional 'longer' innings which he achieved at infrequent intervals through his career were sources of immense satisfaction and huge enjoyment to him.

Statham captained the Lancashire side for three years from 1965 to 1967, and they were three of the most difficult years in the history of the club. The departure of capped and experienced players made it necessary to bring into the senior team, young men who had scarcely made their mark in the second XI, let alone in Championship cricket. The pace bowling could not be faulted, for in Statham himself and Higgs, Lancashire had two attacking opening bowlers, second to none in the country. There were, too, in Lever and Shuttleworth, adequate reserves. The spin bowling, however, was less than adequate, and the main weakness of Lancashire's out-cricket in Statham's years of captaincy was the failure to exploit an advantage once the fast bowlers had made an initial break-through.

The batting was quite frankly immature, and it could be argued with some justification that a batsman-captain if a suitable man had been available would have been better for Lancashire cricket at this particular period. To aggravate the difficulties, experienced capped batsmen, on whom reliance had been placed to give an innings a solid start, too frequently failed to fulfil that function, either through injury or loss of form.

Statham was under no illusions about the immensity of his task when the Committee invited him to take over the captaincy. To him it was a challenge, and it was characteristic of the man that there was never any question of refusal. Throughout his cricketing career he had accepted any challenge that was offered, and it would not have been in his nature to turn his back on this one.

He could promise no sudden transformation, no miracles, no short cut to success. He knew well enough that the road ahead would be hard and fraught with difficulties. He must have been well aware that his main function as Lancashire's captain would be to help the young players to keep their feet in what John Bunyan would have known as the Slough of Despond. It might not be his happy lot to lead them to the Delectable Mountains. As events turned out, it was not, but he left to his successor, Jack Bond, a team, that if it were still rather fragile in batting, was in sight of the foothills of promise at last.

The manner of his going from the first-class scene was again thoroughly characteristic of the man. He had long before decided that he would go whilst there was cricket left in him, and not wait until the day came when, as he bowled, the members in the pavilion might be reflecting sadly on his past greatness. A commercial opportunity presented itself and he gave the Lancashire authorities adequate notice of his intentions, resigning the captaincy at the end of the 1967 season.

He had intended to continue to play until the end of June 1968, but he postponed his final appearance for Lancashire so that he could take part in the 'roses' match at Old Trafford in August, the game that had been chosen as Ken Higgs's benefit match.

This last appearance against Yorkshire was charged with all the drama of his first as a gangling youth, eighteen years before. Lancashire had batted first, and had not fared too happily, but at the end of the day Statham took the Yorkshire batting by the scruff of its neck, shot out three of its prime exponents in ten deliveries and finished the session with 5 wickets for 20 runs in eight overs. His final analysis of 6 for 34 was evidence enough, if any were needed, that the old lion's fangs were still in sharp trim.

After his retirement from first-class cricket Statham received offers from league clubs, but he refused them all, taking the view that, whilst he might always enjoy a battle with rival profession-als, he would certainly not be happy bowling flat out against youngsters starting out on their cricketing careers. He would have hated to feel that he might be the means of depriving teenage batsmen of their appetite for cricket by bowling fast and straight at them on doubtful pitches.

The 'fast and straight' adverbial clause was as characteristic of Statham as the sentiments, for he could bowl no other way. The sentiments were derived from his long experience in the first-class game, particularly as Lancashire's captain, for he had seen the dearth of young talent coming to county cricket from the leagues.

No young man from whatever sphere of cricket he may come could have a finer model than Brian Statham. Not only was he a great bowler and an undemonstrative one, a man of engaging modesty, a hard worker and a trier from the first ball of the day to the last; these qualities added to his wonderful accuracy and impeccable control exemplified all that is best in the summer game.

XXIII

Jack Bond

In the early nineteen-sixties Lancashire cricket plumbed the depths. At various times there were clear indications that all was not well in the team, in the relationship between captain and team, between captain and Committee and between the Committee and the team. Inevitably the performance of the team suffered, and in 1963 members had the unhappy experience of seeing Lancashire slide to penultimate position in the County Championship table.

The captaincy of Cyril Washbrook, a man of firm views and a great believer in firm discipline was followed by that of Bob Barber, a fine young all-rounder who had much to give to Lancashire cricket if only it had been realized soon enough. As it was his full potential was realized with Warwickshire after he had left Old Trafford. An error was made in giving him the captaincy too early. A year or two's more experience of playing under another captain could have made Barber a better leader and possibly ironed out an inherently cautious approach to the problems of captaincy.

His two seasons as captain of Lancashire were unhappy both for him and for his team. He seemed at odds with the Committee, which probably with some justification, considered that he could have bowled himself more than he was wont to do, and there were problems of discipline within the side.

After two seasons he gave way in 1962 to J.R. Blackledge, a club cricketer who may have had more experience of captaincy, but found the leading of a county side vastly different from performing the same function in club cricket. Blackledge lasted only one season and was succeeded by Ken Grieves who had left Old Trafford where he had served many fruitful seasons to take a business appointment, but returned when he was offered the captaincy.

Grieves led the side for two seasons and brought a more positive approach, but when he returned to his business appointment and league cricket, the county side was not noticeably in better heart than when he took over. In point of fact the departure to other counties for one reason or another of such experienced capped players as Wharton, Barber, Marner and Clayton had substantially weakened the side when there was an urgent need to strengthen it. Though the Committee might have viewed one or two of the departures as a cleansing of the Augean Stables, others were serious losses to the club, and all considerably reduced the available playing strength.

There were changes in the Committee also, and among the new members to be elected was Cedric Rhoades who had been a trenchant critic of the former Committee's policies and had viewed with mounting dismay the departure from Old Trafford of so many established players. Rhoades brought to the Committee the intense energy and unremitting concern for Lancashire cricket he had shown so formidably as a critic, and it came as no surprise when, after only a short time as a Committee member, he was elected vice-Chairman and subsequently Chairman.

Brian Statham was under no illusions about the immensity of the task that faced him when he accepted the captaincy in succession to Grieves. Young players were of necessity brought into the side before they were really ready for first-class cricket, and to add to his difficulties some of the capped players who were left and who were expected to provide the batting backbone of the team whilst the younger men were blooded, too often suffered from injuries and loss of form. Though Statham would be the last to claim that he possessed a high proportion of the qualities essential to the make-up of a successful captain, he was popular with the players, and in each of the three seasons in which he led the side before his own retirement Lancashire rose one place in the Championship table. Statham did a magnificent job in forging together the nucleus of a new team for his successor, Jack Bond.

Meanwhile a gust of fresh air was blowing in Committee and Cedric Rhoades was making his presence felt in no uncertain manner. The clarion call went out from Old Trafford. Lancashire cricket must be put back on the map and the county side made a power in the land again.

Jack Bond, who had first played for Lancashire in 1955 had proved a very successful captain of the second XI, with the estimable quality of being able to get the best out of his men.

When he took over the captaincy of the senior team from Brian Statham in 1968, he inherited a side which contained several fine individual players who were consistently playing below their potential, a reflection of the conflict and dissension behind the scenes at Old Trafford. Bond realized the weaknesses in his team, and crystallized his approach to remedy them in two main objectives. Firstly he stressed the importance of the fielding, and made it clear that he was not prepared to consider anyone for a place in the side who was not committed to all-out effort to improve in this crucial and frequently neglected sphere of the game. To this end he preached the gospel of physical fitness, and his players were urged and encouraged by Bond's own example to maintain themselves in good trim. Secondly he emphasized the need for a more positive and assertive approach in Lancashire's cricket, a faster scoring rate, tight field placing and accurate bowling.

The cautiously defensive safety-first approach which had produced no successful results must be shed, and to achieve this objective he knew that the fears of his men that they might lose their places if they failed through trying to play more positive cricket must be resolved. He had a staunch ally in the new Chairman, Cedric Rhoades whom he described as a one-hundred per cent player's man and for the first time for many years Lancashire's cricketers felt that the Committee did really care about them, their problems and their futures. Apathy which had been carried from the pavilion onto the field disappeared, and in the first season of Bond's leadership Lancashire rose to sixth place in the County Championship table. The resurgence had begun.

Dwindling gate receipts and a decline in membership in the lean years had brought home to the Committee the necessity of having a successful team for the public would not pay to watch a struggling one. Most counties had brought into their sides established players from overseas who had made their mark in Test cricket in their own countries. These players, besides strengthening their county teams, brought a new spirit with them, and by their uninhibited approach to the game provided the sort of entertaining cricket which the public was prepared to pay to see.

Farokh Engineer, an Indian Test wicket-keeper-batsman was signed on an immediate registration, and Clive Lloyd, a West Indian Test all-rounder entered into a contract by which, after a

M

year's residential qualification, he would be available to play county cricket in 1969.

Engineer and Lloyd must surely have been the best pair of 'imports' in the county cricket of their time. Engineer's brilliant wicket-keeping and his zest for the game gave the Lancashire fielding a keener edge and raised the performances of his colleagues in this department to new peaks of achievement. Clive Lloyd's reputation as one of the greatest fieldsmen in the world was established before he came to Old Trafford, and he brought to the Lancashire out-cricket a feline grace and agility that saved countless runs and delighted crowds all over the country.

The nucleus of a side strong enough to restore Lancashire's fortunes was now established and under Bond's leadership the renaissance was launched. In 1969, the year of its inception, Lancashire won the new John Player League championship, and by their shrewd pacing of an innings, tight fielding and accurate bowling Bond and his men proved themselves masters of limited-overs cricket.

Unhappily in this year Lancashire's position in the County Championship table dropped from sixth to fifteenth. This was a disappointment, but in extenuation it could be pointed out that over one-third of the total playing time had been lost through inclement weather and in several of the early games neither side had been able to start a second innings. Allowing for these disadvantages, however, the scoring had not been as quick as Bond could have wished. Before the start of the 1970 season he stressed the need for a faster run-rate to increase batting bonus points and provide a sounder springboard for victory.

His call was answered with a right good will; not only did Lancashire rise to third place in the County Championship with double the number of batting bonus points, they also won the John Player League Championship for the second year in succession and the Gillette Cup for the first time. It was Lancashire's best season for years. Under Bond's positive leadership and tactful understanding his players had welded together into a formidable side. The bowling still needed strengthening for there was a lack of penetration once the openers were off and it was difficult to dismiss a side twice on a good wicket, but all the players made important contributions to the success of the team and the younger players performed well when Test calls and injuries took away senior men. The crowds flocked back to Old Trafford, particularly for the Sunday League games, and when Lancashire beat Yorkshire in August to make the title theirs, 28,000 people watched the cricket. The 1971 season was a little less successful. Third position was maintained in the County Championship, but the John Player League title was yielded to Worcestershire. It was in the Gillette Cup cricket this year, however, that Lancashire won their proudest honours and captured the imagination of the public in a series of brilliant victories. In all of them the guiding influence and tactical flair of Jack Bond was conspicuous, never more so than in the semi-final with Gloucestershire at Old Trafford and in the final with Kent at Lord's.

The semi-final drew a capacity crowd and the gates were closed with many thousands more locked outside the ground. In their sixty overs Gloucestershire scored 229 for 6, but rain had delayed the restart of play after lunch and with the shades of night fast falling Lancashire were still 67 runs short of their target with 4 wickets in hand and 14 overs remaining. When the light began to fail, Bond, who was at the wicket, was asked by the umpires whether he wished to play to a finish that night or continue the innings next morning.

Bond knew that to defer a finish until the following morning would bring a refreshed Gloucestershire pace attack into action, and the Lancashire lower order could find it considerably more difficult to get the runs they needed for victory. He elected, therefore, to continue and the innings proceeded in deepening gloom which added to the batsmen's problems.

Simmons laid about to good effect, but when he was out 27 runs were still needed with only five overs remaining to be bowled. It seemed that Lancashire's hopes were fading with the light and that Bond's calculated gamble had gone awry. Not a soul dared to leave the vast arena, and at this crucial moment of the game the readiness of each and every one of the Lancashire players to produce extra effort was memorably exemplified in the performance of David Hughes, the batsman at the opposite end.

Before the 56th over began, Bond, so the story goes, walked down the wicket and said to Hughes 'Don't go daft. Take things as they come.' And the doughty Hughes replied, 'Alright, skipper. If I can see 'em, I can hit 'em.'

The record of that over bowled by Mortimore has passed into

Lancashire cricket history. His six balls were hit for 6,4,2,2,4,6. Bond made the winning hit in the next over as the hands of the pavilion clock were approaching 9 o'clock and the street lights were being lit around the ground.

In the final at Lord's, a game of absorbing cut-and-thrust, in which first one side and then the other gained the advantage, Bond at another crucial moment produced a splendid individual piece of cricket that finally turned the game Lancashire's way.

Kent were chasing a Lancashire score of 224 for 7 and initially they had fared none too well, losing half their wickets for 105. Then Asif Iqbal, a fine all-rounder took command of the innings, showing such a complete disregard for the Lancashire bowling that with 4 wickets and 6 overs remaining he had brought Kent to within 28 runs of victory. It seemed impossible to set a field to contain him, and whilst he remained at the wicket a Kent win looked a distinct probability.

When Asif had scored 89 there came the moment which decided the match. Simmons was bowling to a strong on-side field, and Asif made room to off-drive, hitting the ball cleanly and with telling force seemingly well wide of extra-cover. Bond, who was fielding there, seemed to hesitate (he explained later that he had thought it a bump-ball), but he suddenly took off, plucked the ball unbelievably out of the air and held on to it as he fell, rolling over and over on the ground. It was a catch in a thousand; it had the effect at once of removing the main threat to Lancashire's hopes of victory and of taking the steam out of the Kent innings. The remaining wickets fell for the addition of only 3 runs and Lancashire had won the match and retained the Gillette Cup. No other player could have more appropriately made the catch than the captain whose purposeful leadership had played such a vital part in his team's success.

Bond, a native of Kearsley, a barren, unattractive area of the hinterland betwixt Manchester and Bolton, was educated at Bolton School and played much of his early cricket in the Bolton League. Though he first played for Lancashire in 1955 it was not until 1961 that he was awarded his county cap. Whilst small of stature he was a naturally aggressive batsman who did not relish being tied down and was not afraid to hit the ball over the close field. In addition he was a fearless fieldsman, specializing in his early days with the county side at backward short-leg or leg-slip.

In 1961 he scored 1700 runs at an average of 36 and the

following year he was Lancashire's most prolific scorer with more than 2100 runs, averaging 37. In 1963, however, he had the ill fortune to have his wrist broken by a ball from Wesley Hall, the West Indian fast bowler and he played in only eleven matches that season and only one in 1964.

He never recovered the batting form of his two vintage seasons, but with typical courage and true Lancashire grit he fought back to establish himself as a reliable middle-order batsman with the valuable faculty for shoring up an innings when things were going badly. His inspiration and example to the younger players and his whole-hearted commitment to Lancashire cricket brought in 1968 his appointment to succeed Brian Statham as captain of the county side.

There were inevitably those who questioned the advisability of appointing to the captaincy an unassuming man whose salad days were behind him. Their doubts were soon set at rest. From the start Bond showed his true metal and revealed in addition to his many other fine qualities a shrewd cricketing brain.

At first he had to feel his way cautiously for he was leading a young, relatively inexperienced team. He could not afford to lose too many games for to have done so would have destroyed confidence at the outset. The way in which he gave his players a belief in their own abilities, and by harnessing the various abilities into an integrated team, restored the fortunes of Lancashire cricket was a fair measure of the man.

A modest fellow in all conscience, a man who led by example rather than by stern discipline, Bond gave all the credit for Lancashire's cricket resurgence to his players. Each of them, he contended, apart from his individual cricketing ability made an important contribution to the morale, purpose and attitude of the side. He would say that he had an easy team to captain because most of the players grew up under him when he was in charge of the second XI. Watching the Lancashire players move to their positions in the field, frequently without direction might have caused the onlooker to think that Bond's assertion could well be true, until he appreciated by the runs saved that the precise positionings had been worked out expertly by a cool, clinical brain.

In 1972 he led Lancashire to their third successive Gillette Cup Final victory when they beat Warwickshire by 4 wickets in another memorable match. At the end of that season, feeling that his playing days were coming to an end, he announced his retirement and was appointed to the coaching staff.

In his playing career at Old Trafford he had scored nearly 12,000 runs for Lancashire and hit thirteen centuries, his highest score 157 against Hampshire in 1962. His five centuries that season included one in each of the 'roses' matches, 144 at Headingley and 109 at Old Trafford. Not many Lancashire batsmen have achieved that distinction against the Old Enemy.

But Jack Bond's services as a player to his beloved Lancashire will not ultimately be measured in terms of runs scored or saved. By his inspiration and example, his belief in his players and his encouragement of them to believe in themselves, he brought after dark days at Old Trafford a fine bloom to the red rose.

His contribution to Lancashire cricket, however, was not yet finished. After a brief spell as coach he received an invitation from Trent Bridge to take over the Notts captaincy after the departure of Gary Sobers. It was, as he afterwards admitted, a mistake. Old Anno Domini was catching up on him and he did not stay long. He left to take up a coaching and groundsman's appointment at a school in the Isle of Man. Towards the end of the summer of 1979 when the fortunes of Lancashire cricket, which had been declining alarmingly since the days of his captaincy, had reached a nadir and the county side was in poor spirit, he accepted an invitation from the Committee to become team manager. So, in Lancashire's time of need Jack Bond returned to Old Trafford. Another renaissance was required, a near miracle might have to be worked. Certain it was that if he could not bring back past glories it would not be for want of dedicated effort, application and inspiration.

XXIV

Farokh Engineer

A red rose of darker hue, Farokh Engineer graced Old Trafford for eight summers which were the happier for his presence. He was born in Bombay in 1938 of Parsee parents, made his first-class cricket debut in his homeland in 1958 and his first appearance in Test cricket against England at Kanpur in the 1961/62 series. He toured England for the first time in 1967 with the Nawab of Pataudi's side and joined Lancashire on an immediate registration a year later. He made his first appearance for the county against Kent at Canterbury, but that first season in English cricket was disappointing. Engineer rarely demonstrated the batting qualities that had prompted the Lancashire committee to engage him as a wicket-keeper-batsman. It is conceivable that experimenting with his batting position did not help his form or his confidence.

He batted at No. 5 in a Gillette Cup game at Trent Bridge early in the season and was run-out for 10. At No. 4 in the county game at Canterbury he was bowled for 15 in the first innings and caught at the wicket for 1 in the second. Back to No. 5 he went at the Oval, to be run-out for 23; at No. 4 again against Notts he failed to score, and still at No. 4 at Lord's he was dismissed for one and nought. When Middlesex came to Old Trafford he was dropped in the order to No. 7 and scored 7 and 10. Thereupon someone, with the fire of inspiration within him, must have remembered that he had opened for India in Test matches, and so it came to pass that he was called upon to open the innings against Sussex at Eastbourne. Sadly, there was no improvement – 1 in the first innings and 4 in the second. At Southport Derbyshire dismissed him for a single in each innings and at Cambridge he suffered the traumatic experience of hitting his wicket. Apart from scoring 70 against Somerset at Old Trafford and 54 against Warwickshire at Aigburth there was little for members to enthuse over in his batting. In that first season he had 62 victims at the wicket, but these figures did not appease the Pavilion critics who had expected a batsman-wicket-keeper rather than a wicket-keeper-batsman.

The shrewder judges knew, however that better times were to come. In the next season he failed by only 48 to complete a thousand runs; had he not missed four games through injury he would almost certainly have achieved that distinction. He made his first century for the county (103 not out) against Glamorgan at Swansea, and to show that his wicket-keeping was not being neglected he took eight catches when Lancashire played Somerset at Taunton. In Lancashire's second innings in the same match he also achieved the dubious distinction of being bowled by Virgin, a very occasional bowler and the ninth to be tried by the cider county in that particular match.

Virgin's success at Taunton epitomized Farokh Engineer's approach to batting. He was essentially a swashbuckler, a Parsee pirate (though the Parsees, I know are not renowned for piracy), a pirate whose flashing cutlass was a bat. His swashbuckling made him vulnerable to almost any bowler in cricket who could turn an arm over, but on the other hand the best in the game were banged against the sightscreen or lifted into the tea-tent when he was at his most destructive. An innings of his, one Sunday afternoon at Buxton, where he narrowly missed scoring the fastest 50 of the season in a John Player League game, is still spoken of with awe in that Derbyshire spa town. Dedicated topers fled from a canvas bar when a ball, propelled ferociously from Engineer's bat, hurtled into their midst like a meteorite from outer space. It is said that one gentleman suffered the shock and mortification of having his pint hurled from his grasp and his glass smashed to smithereens, the beverage scattered and wasted. That gentleman can still be recognized in Buxton by a now permanent nervous twitch. True connoisseurs of the game will not be sympathetic, I fancy. What was he doing inside instead of outside the beer-tent whilst Engineer was despatching his thunderbolts to all points of the compass? Had he been where he should have been, he could then have seen what was coming and taken the appropriate avoiding action.

As a batsman a lot depended on Farokh's mood, though he was not so moody as the great George Gunn, who was reputed once to have thrown away his wicket at Cardiff because they took lunch there at 2 o'clock and George's stomach was not conditioned to having its 'vittles' later than 1.30 p.m. His captain could never rely on Farokh to salvage a lost cause or put down an anchor. He could be (and often was) out to the most outrageous, unorthodox strokes, yet strode cheerfully from the wicket in the sure knowledge that there was always another day.

When keeping wicket he seemed always on the move, and there was usually, when the ball had passed the bat and was in his gloves, a final flourish with the ball held against a stump, a warning to the batsman that he was hawk-eyed, vigilant, ready for a stumping, should the back foot be lifted the merest fraction of an inch. Often a bail was removed, and I imagine many an umpire has cursed him, silently or perhaps more publicly, when he has had to run in from square-leg to adjust the wicket. It was impossible to be really angry with him for he always looked so apologetic for his zest, and indeed the practice gradually became established among the less rigorous of the white-coated brother-hood to leave the adjustment to Farokh himself. A pirate maybe, but a trusty pirate.

To his bowling colleagues he could be both infuriating and inspiring. He might miss the most simple of catches and snap up the most impossible, leaping to left or right, perhaps finishing up asprawl, but with the ball held triumphantly in his glove.

On and off the field he was a 'character' and a credit to the game. He was forever chattering to whoever might listen, and he chatted alike to those who might not. As a Parsee he must have known all about the Towers of Silence, but silence was never part of his make-up. There was always something to be cheerful about and he was ever eager to share his cheer with others.

Figures sometimes give the measure of a cricketer or of a man, sometimes not. In his first-class career, in all matches, Farokh Engineer scored 13,000 runs at an average of 29 and claimed over 800 victims at the wicket. For Lancashire, in first-class matches he scored nearly 6,000 runs and took nearly 500 at the wicket. It should not be forgotten that in Test matches for India he scored hundreds against England and West Indies. The records reveal that as a bowler he took 1 wicket for 117 runs.

He rather fancied himself as a leg-break bowler, and indeed at a Weston-super-Mare Festival I once saw him turning over his wrist, bowling to some youngsters before the start of a day's play. Whether the deliveries would have troubled an experienced batsman is open to doubt. I do know, however that the boys were enjoying it all immensely and I am certain that Farokh was.

XXV

Clive Lloyd

No player has made the same impact on Lancashire cricket as Clive Hubert Lloyd. Cricketers have a perverse humour in calling their colleagues by the most unlikely of their baptismal names and Clive Lloyd has always been known as 'Big Hubert' to his team-mates. Big he certainly is, 6ft 4½ inches in height and weighing 14 stones, yet in the field something of a stoop and a lope rarely give a full impression of the immensity of his strength. To watch him bat in the full flow of his authority and power is to experience all the exhilarating skills and dominance of a master batsman. The heaviest bat in cricket (over 3 lbs in weight), his long reach, perfect timing and aggressive instinct have made him a feared adversary to all bowlers.

The bowler, however, always has a chance with Clive Lloyd. At the start of an innings he often seems fallible, his bat sounding as if it were made of hardboard, rather than of solid willow. Once he has gauged the pace of the wicket and the set of the field he will begin to unleash his strokes with his shrewd instinct, judgement and panache. Consciously the stroke-player does not think in terms of hundreds. He is usually content to play his shots and let the runs come. Thus Clive Lloyd has not made the number of centuries that cricket's records accord to less gifted but more dogged and concentrative batsmen. Often he has been out when a century has seemed his for the taking.

The prospect of seeing Clive Lloyd in action has, in his cricketing career, brought the crowds surging through the turnstiles on every ground in the country. The tremendous power with which he hits the ball and the immaculate timing have brought joy and excitement to cricket-lovers all over the world. In a felicitous phrase from one of his commentaries of a hit of Lloyd's that sent the ball far out of the ground, John Arlott spoke of the batsman, 'not so much hitting the ball as waving it goodbye.'

In his earlier years in cricket Lloyd patrolled the covers when his side was fielding like a hungry panther. His speed, long reach, safe hands and scorchingly accurate returns and the large stretches of ground he covered often gave the impression that the fielding side had an extra man. Until operations to both his knees reduced his mobility he was reckoned one of the greatest cover-points of all time. Before the knee surgery he was a useful bowler at brisk medium pace, often brought on to break a stubborn partnership or bowl economically in limited-over cricket.

Clive Hubert was born in Georgetown, Guyana on August 31st, 1944. He was educated in his native town and at the age of 12, whilst trying to separate two fighting schoolmates, he received a blow in the eye. His eyesight was affected and he has been obliged to wear spectacles ever since. Like many another West Indian boy he was early attracted to cricket and learned the game by playing with older boys, among them his cousin Lance Gibbs who was later to take 312 Test wickets for West Indies. As left-hand batsman and right-arm leg-break bowler Lloyd first played for Guyana in his late teens.

In 1967 he came to England to play as professional for Haslingden in the Lancashire League. Not only the League bowlers suffered the summary consequences of the blows from the immense bat. Haslingden members recall with many a chuckle how Lloyd once felled his batting partner who turned his back and took the full force of a straight drive on his rump. In League cricket Lloyd abandoned his leg-breaks for more utilitarian medium pace which he was subsequently to bowl in Test and county cricket.

Lloyd accepted a contract with Lancashire when his Haslingden engagement expired and in his first full county season he drew the crowds wherever the team played. This exciting new cricketer, then in his 26th year, had acquired from his experiences in English cricket an increasing maturity to add to his natural talents. He enjoyed his cricket and the spectators enjoyed watching him play it. At this time Lancashire were the kings of limited-over cricket. No county can match their record in Gillette Cup matches; Lloyd played a considerable part in that success over the years and when Gillette ended their sponsorship in 1980, he was awarded the 'Man of the Series' trophy as the player who had made the highest contribution.

Lancashire's county championship fortunes in Lloyd's time at

Old Trafford have not been so successful, though he has played a dominant part when he has been available. His runs for Lancashire, at the time of writing, include 28 centuries, six against Yorkshire, a Lancashire 'roses' record. In all first-class cricket he has hit 70 centuries. An innings of 201 not out for West Indies against Glamorgan in 1976 was made in 120 minutes, equalling in time a Gilbert Jessop record set up in 1903. For West Indies in Tests he has scored over 6,000 runs, highest score 242 not out. Apart from his Test and county achievements Lloyd has scored runs all over the world and played a spectacular part in international limited-over cricket.

Though he had been West Indies captain since 1974, and would have been pleased to lead Lancashire had the captaincy been offered him, the Committee was always aware of his other commitment to his national team which could not be smoothly reconciled with county continuity. Championship success eluded Lancashire and at last in 1981, Clive Lloyd became captain of his adopted county. Jack Bond, a shrewd cricket manager, had seen the need to introduce younger blood to the senior side more quickly and he required the knowledge, experience and maturity of Lloyd to help him. With two or three seasons left to him in first-class cricket Clive Lloyd accepted the challenge with relish. What the two wise men make of the talent available remains to be seen; at the end of the 1982 season there was promise enough.

I imagine that if precedent for former West Indies Test captains is followed Clive Lloyd will in due time receive a knighthood. Will it be as 'Sir Clive', or 'Sir Hubert', that we in Lancashire will remember him? He will then have achieved every honour that cricket can bestow, But I have the feeling that the recent conferment on him of the degree of Master of Arts (honoris causa) by Manchester University will give him most pleasure. Cricket is an art in itself and for the zest and skill with which he played it and the entertainment he has given to so many, Clive Lloyd is well worthy of the title of Master.

INDEX

(Chapters are indicated by Roman numerals).